I0802042

TPBA Play-Based TPBI
TPBC

Read, Play, and Learn!

Storybook Activities for Young Children

Module 4

This is one module of a total collection of eight. The following are the other seven modules included in Collection 1:

Module 1: *The Kissing Hand*
Module 2: *Somebody and the Three Blairs*
Module 3: *Picking Apples & Pumpkins*
Module 5: *The Knight and the Dragon*
Module 6: *Abiyoyo*
Module 7: *Night Tree*
Module 8: *The Snowy Day*

In addition, there is a Collection 2 of ***Read, Play, and Learn!*** The following are the eight modules included:

Module 9: *A Porcupine Named Fluffy*
Module 10: *First Flight*
Module 11: *Friends*
Module 12: *The Three Billy Goats Gruff*
Module 13: *The Three Little Javelinas*
Module 14: *A Rainbow of Friends*
Module 15: *Franklin Has a Sleepover*
Module 16: *The Rainbow Fish*

Other products available in the TPBA *Play-Based* TPBI TPBC system include the following:

- *Teacher's Guide for Read, Play, and Learn! Storybook Activities for Young Children*
- *Transdisciplinary Play-Based Assessment: A Functional Approach to Working with Young Children, Revised Edition*
- *Transdisciplinary Play-Based Intervention: Guidelines for Developing Meaningful Curricula for Young Children*
- *And You Thought They Were Just Playing: Transdisciplinary Play-Based Assessment* (videotape)
- *Observing Kassandra: A Transdisciplinary Play-Based Assessment of a Child with Severe Disabilities* (videotape)

Look inside the back cover for ordering information.

·P A U L·H·
BROOKES
PUBLISHING CO.

Baltimore · London · Toronto · Sydney

The Transdisciplinary Play-Based Curriculum from Toni Linder

TPBA Play-Based TPBI
TPBC

Read, Play, and Learn!
Storybook Activities for Young Children

Module 4

Based on The Little Old Lady Who Was Not Afraid of Anything

Module developed by

Toni W. Linder

This module was field-tested and reviewed by Regina "Patsy" Boughan, Katie Greer, and Karen T. Harmon.

Paul H. Brookes Publishing Co.
Post Office Box 10624
Baltimore, Maryland 21285-0624

www.brookespublishing.com

Typeset by A.W. Bennett, Inc., Hartland, Vermont.
Manufactured in the United States of America by
Printing Corporation of America, Baltimore, Maryland.

Paul H. Brookes Publishing Co. thanks HarperCollins for permission to base this module on *The Little Old Lady Who Was Not Afraid of Anything,* by Linda Williams. Jacket art copyright © 1996 by Megan Lloyd; used by permission of HarperCollins Publishers.

For information about Toni W. Linder, Ed.D., and the module developers, please refer to pages vii–viii of the *Teacher's Guide for Read, Play, and Learn! Storybook Activities for Young Children.*

1-55766-406-4

CONTENTS

HOW TO USE *READ, PLAY, AND LEARN!*

Think how much more motivated to read children would be if reading stories and using print materials enriched and enlivened their play. The booklet you are holding in your hands is one of several modules in ***Read, Play, and Learn!***, a play-based curriculum designed not only to enhance emergent literacy skills but also to promote growth across all of the areas of development important for a young child.

The Curriculum

A storybook-based curriculum is not a new concept. Teachers and child care providers have, after all, been using books as an important piece of their programming for centuries. What is different about this curriculum is the integration of all areas of development into a full spectrum of activities, all relating to one book, with accompanying modifications and adaptations to meet the needs of *all* children in the class. ***Read, Play, and Learn!*** encourages children to *actively participate* in a *literacy-rich* environment of *playful* activities that foster *cognitive, language, social,* and *motor* development.

Module Format

Each module of ***Read, Play, and Learn!***, using the magic of a different storybook, provides 2 weeks of engaging, theme-based activities to help children learn. This module, like all of the others, has the following sections:

1. *The Story:* A brief retelling or summary of the picture book, with information on where to get the book
2. *The Planning Sheets:* Charts for at-a-glance reference to all of the suggested activities to use for the 2 weeks
3. *Vocabulary:* A list of the key words and concepts, including labels, action words, and descriptors, to which the children can be introduced with this story
4. *Materials:* A list of the toys, playthings, equipment, food, supplies, and other items needed for the module
5. *Areas/Centers:* A description of 10 days of different activities for each area or center in the classroom, plus suggested modifications for the sensorimotor, functional, and symbolic levels of learning (described in the next section)
6. *How to Involve Families:* Recommendations to help keep family members or other caregivers informed, including sample letters to send home
7. *More Suggestions:* Alternative storybooks and other activities (e.g., songs, fingerplays, resources, software) that can be used with the module

In most instances, you will probably find there are more activities than you will use. This overplanning is intentional so that you can select activities that match the interests, abilities, and educational and developmental needs of the children you serve.

The Play Areas

The "centers," or areas of the classroom, include places for reading the story, dramatizing the story, and engaging in sensory and motor play; a literacy center; an art area; and sites for science and math activities, floor play, table play, outdoor fun, woodworking, and snacktime. The centers may be distinct or may serve multiple purposes. All centers may be set up in the room simultaneously, or you may choose to generate only a few of the areas at a time. Adding to or changing the centers for each of the modules to maintain children's high level of involvement is encouraged. For more background on structuring your classroom, refer to the *Teacher's Guide.*

The *Teacher's Guide*

Be sure to read the ***Read, Play, and Learn!*** *Teacher's Guide* before using any of the modules. (If you do not already have your copy, ordering information is included on page 74.) The *Teacher's Guide* describes the foundations of the curriculum, provides instruction in using the curriculum with children of different ages and ability levels, offers suggestions for classroom set-up, reviews the stages of literacy development, and helps you get family members or other caregivers involved. You will also find helpful information on weekly planning, team use of the modules, and sequencing of modules to correspond with holidays and seasons of the year.

The Children

Read, Play, and Learn! has been designed primarily for children between the ages of 3 and 6. You will find it effective, though, with children in your classroom whose developmental age ranges from 1 to 6 years old. As you progress through each module, you will find that levels of learning are discussed for the activities in each play area or center. By following the tips in these sections, you can adjust the suggested activities to the needs of the individual learners in your classroom. The *Teacher's Guide* and other products from Toni Linder (1993a, 1993b) will help you learn to identify the level of learning each child is ready for.

1. *Sensorimotor:* At this earliest level of development, children are learning about concrete meanings through physical manipulation of the environment around them. They are more interested in the sounds of words being read, pictures in a book, and the concrete associations of the words that are meaningful to them. This stage roughly corresponds to the cognitive and language levels of children functioning from early infancy to about 18 months of age. This stage is also called the *exploratory* level.
2. *Functional:* At this second level, children are listening and watching, imitating, relating, and beginning to sequence ideas and actions. They are interested in listening to the story but are still more interested in talking about the pictures than telling the story per se. This level coincides approximately with children functioning from about 18 months to 3 years of age.
3. *Symbolic:* When children become interested in learning and representing their understanding through a variety of representational and symbolic

means, including fantasy play, storytelling, music, dance, art, drawing, and print, they have reached the symbolic level. Children at this level, typically 3 years of age or older, become interested in the print in the picture book, the story sequence, and the telling of the story.

Why Should I Use *Read, Play, and Learn!?*

The advantages of ***Read, Play, and Learn!*** are many. The use of the same storybook over 2 weeks (it can be extended to a longer period of time if desired) allows repeated encounters with themes and concepts and the modification, adaptation, and generalization of skills related to those ideas across time and from school to home. The reiteration of concepts and themes provides opportunities for understanding in multiple ways. The development of projects allows children to work at their own pace. Repeated exposure to activities builds memory skills. Actions, events, characters, language structures, and vocabulary are increasingly understood, retained, and applied. In short, each story, and its related activities, serves as the stimulus for discussion, play, exploration, investigation, dramatization, creative expression, socialization, and emerging literacy development.

Now, to Get Started . . .

You will first want to familiarize yourself with the content of the *Teacher's Guide* and several of the modules. Then, choose a sequence of modules that makes the most sense for the time of year you are starting to use the curriculum and the children with whom you are working.

Read through the complete module. If you do not already have a copy of the storybook, then obtain one. Each story associated with a module is a popular children's book available in most bookstores and libraries, but if you are not able to find the exact book, then at the back of the module you will find a list of other books that you can substitute.

Refer to the Planning Sheets to see how the storybook becomes the basis for each day's activities. Then, gather the materials you will need, and plan how you want to set up your classroom. Everything you will need is identified in the Materials section of the module.

Now you are ready to use the daily suggestions in the areas/centers of the module to make ***Read, Play, and Learn!*** work in your classroom or child care center. The *Teacher's Guide* will give you more information on the importance of starting each day with the reading of the story followed by an acting out or dramatization. Each day you will embellish the reading and involve the children more; ideas for how to do this across the 2 weeks are included in the module. Then you can choose from among the many descriptions of specific activities for each area or center you set up. You may follow the Planning Sheets exactly or you may use the Planning Sheet Master in the Appendix at the end of the *Teacher's Guide* to modify and adapt the storybook modules for the children in your classroom. Each of these sections of the module is followed by tips on how to modify the activities so that all children benefit whether they are sensorimotor, functional, or symbolic learners. You'll be able to teach or supervise children in groups but still individualize the instruction to suit each child.

The *Teacher's Guide* includes suggestions for adaptations and modifications to use the curriculum with children with disabilities or special needs. By using

Read, Play, and Learn! in conjunction with Toni Linder's other products, *Transdisciplinary Play-Based Assessment* and *Transdisciplinary Play-Based Intervention* (1993a, 1993b), you'll make your classroom an inclusive learning environment. (To order either of these books, with more information on individualized family service plans and individualized education programs, refer to page 74.)

Before you are actually under way, be sure to read the important section on involving families. You'll want to let the care providers of the children you see each day know what story is being discussed in school so that learning can extend to the home. By sending home a letter of explanation and perhaps even a modified version of the Planning Sheets for the story, parents can work on vocabulary, themes, and concepts at home. The more parents know about what is happening during the day, the more they will have to talk about with their children. Some families will even go to the library or bookstore to have a copy of the storybook at home.

Have Fun! So, turn your classroom into a place for dialogue, discourse, and discovery, not just question and response. Modify and create; inspire and stimulate. Have fun, and the children you teach or care for will, too!

References

Linder, T.W. (1993a). *Transdisciplinary play-based assessment: A functional approach to working with young children* (Rev. ed.). Baltimore: Paul H. Brookes Publishing Co.

Linder, T.W. (1993b). *Transdisciplinary play-based intervention: Guidelines for developing a meaningful curriculum for young children.* Baltimore: Paul H. Brookes Publishing Co.

THE STORY

The Little Old Lady Who Was Not Afraid of Anything, written by Linda Williams and illustrated by Megan Lloyd, is a book that fits nicely with Halloween. The story is about a little old lady who sets out to gather herbs, spices, seeds, and nuts from the forest. It is dark when she starts home. She soon discovers that she is being followed by a pair of shoes that go "CLOMP, CLOMP." She is not afraid but hurries on. Subsequently, she is followed by a pair of pants, a shirt, two gloves, a hat, and a scary pumpkin head, all of which make frightening noises. They chase her home and try again to scare her, but she is not to be frightened. Instead, she recommends that they stay in her garden and scare her crows away.

This is a fun book for children because of the repetition of the sounds and actions that the various clothes and objects make (CLOMP, CLOMP; WIGGLE, WIGGLE; SHAKE, SHAKE; CLAP, CLAP; NOD, NOD; BOO, BOO) as they follow the old lady. The children soon begin to remember the associated noises and can cheerfully render them as the story progresses.

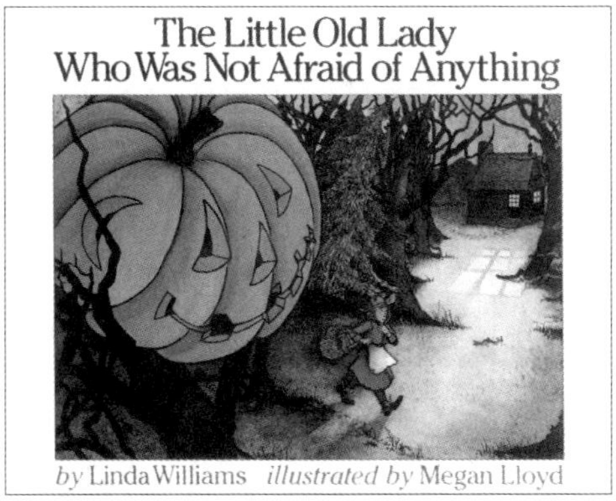

Title:	*The Little Old Lady Who Was Not Afraid of Anything*
Author:	Linda Williams
Illustrator:	Megan Lloyd
Publisher:	HarperCollins
Price:	$5.95* for papercover $15.00* for hardcover

Try your local bookstore or library to obtain this book.
*Suggested retail price

Play-Based Curriculum Planning Sheet: Storybook Activities

Date: Week One **Theme (optional):** Bravery **Book title (optional):** The Little Old Lady Who Was Not Afraid of Anything

Play area	Monday	Tuesday	Wednesday	Thursday	Friday
Reading the Story	Read the story. Hide all of the props behind you, and bring them out one by one as they appear in the story.	Repeat the actions from the previous day. Have an extra set of props to give to one child as that part of the story is read.	Read the story. Hand out two sets of props to two children. Have the children who are assisting sit near you.	Repeat reading the story with enough props so that each child gets a prop. Begin to omit the sound or action to see if the children can fill in the blanks.	Before reading and telling the story again, let one or two children share their books made in the Literacy Center.
Dramatic Play: Theme Area	You will first need to dramatize the story. Incorporate the props into the dramatization in various ways.	You can support the children in acting out the story by prompting the lines from the script.	Repeat having the children act out the story. Add herbs and nuts along the path for the old lady to gather.	Continue with the dramatization and the script. Have the children take turns acting out the clothing parts.	Repeat the dramatization and the script. You may alter the path so that the old lady needs to go down a winding path.
Literacy Center	Make labels for the Dramatic Play: Theme Area. Label the children's footprints made in the Art Area with their names.	Make a book of clothing. Have the children cut out pictures of clothing from catalogs and paste them onto pieces of paper.	Finish making the books from the previous day. The children can make a cover, staple all of the pages and the cover together, and then make up a title.	Draw or find pictures that make the children scared. Create an interactive storyboard.	Have the children dictate a story about something scary. Repeat the interactive storyboard.
Science and Math Center	Study different herbs and spices under a magnifying glass. Tape or paste samples onto a piece of paper. Display the samples.	Help the children carve a pumpkin on which a face was drawn in the Art Area. Let the children clean out the pumpkin.	Have each child take off one of his or her shoes to compare and determine whose is the largest, smallest, and so forth.	Weigh a pair of adult's shoes and a pair of children's shoes. Compare the weights.	Continue to measure and weigh the children's shoes and make comparisons. Introduce new concepts.
Art Area	Make a long path out of newsprint. Have the children make footprints on the path with paint.	Bring in old clothing, and let the children paint designs on them. They may use a variety of tools to make their designs.	Hang clothing on the wall. Tape a large piece of paper to the wall under the clothing. Have the children paint a mural to match the clothing.	Continue working on the mural. Set a pumpkin next to the easel for the children to look at and attempt to paint on the picture.	Continue painting on the mural and on the easel. Let the children experiment with making prints on waxed paper or construction paper with sponges dipped in paint.
Sensory Area	Place dirt in the sand and water table as well as tools and different types of beans and seeds.	Add the garden labels made in the Literacy Center to the garden. Make scarecrows by stuffing old clothes with straw.	The children can dig up the seeds that they planted 2 days before, place them back in the bag, and start the process over.	Add a large box to the end of the path in which the old lady can find seeds, herbs, corn, and so forth.	Repeat the previous day's activities.
Motor Area	Sing a song, and do a fingerplay.	Play slow music. Give the children scarves to wave in the air. Move like trees in the wind.	Use different instruments to accompany loud, pounding music to pretend you are mad, worried, frightened, and so forth.	Have the children use the instruments they made as well as real instruments to make scary noises.	Play Old Lady Says.

Play-Based Curriculum Planning Sheet: Storybook Activities

Date: Week One **Theme (optional):** Bravery **Book title (optional):** The Little Old Lady Who Was Not Afraid of Anything

Play area	Monday	Tuesday	Wednesday	Thursday	Friday
Floor Play	The children can use large blocks to build the old lady's house or a fence around the garden. Lay out puzzles and switch toys.	Legos and other small blocks can be put out for the children to build a miniature scenario of the story. Add small characters and items.	Repeat the miniature scenario. You should need to facilitate less than the previous day.	Repeat the miniature scenario. Play the Shoe Hunt game.	Repeat the miniature scenario. Repeat the Shoe Hunt game.
Table Play	Make puppet scarecrows out of Popsicle sticks and paper.	Repeat the previous day's activity. The children can make little old lady puppets if they want. Make a paper bag head for the scarecrow.	Make sock puppet scarecrows.	Repeat making sock or Popsicle puppets. Make a theater out of a box for the children to reenact the story with their puppets.	Photocopy and cut out different pieces of paper. Have the children stick flannel or Velcro to the paper and use on a flannel board to retell the story.
Outdoor Play	Play the Walk, Stop, and Run game. Free play.	Repeat the Walk, Stop, and Run game. This time let the children take turns shouting out the commands. Free play.	Hide small, plastic pumpkins around the playground, and let the children search for them. Free play.	Hang a clothesline outside. Have the children hang clothing with clothespins. The children will enjoy this over and over again. Free play.	Repeat the hanging of the clothes on the clothesline. Free play.
Snack	Oral motor: The children look in small mirrors at their teeth. Snack: Herb cream cheese and crackers and apple juice	Oral motor: Repeat examining their mouths and teeth in the mirror and making toothless smiles. Snack: Toasted pumpkin seeds and water	Oral motor: Sing a song. Add finger movements. Snack: Creamed corn and milk	Oral motor: Have the children use their lips and tongues to make sound effects. Snack: Herb cream cheese and crackers and lemonade	Oral motor: Repeat the lip and tongue movements that go with the actions of the story. Snack: Cinnamon rice cakes and apple juice
Books and Music					
Software					

TPBA Play-Based TPBI TPBC

Play-Based Curriculum Planning Sheet: Storybook Activities

Date: Week Two **Theme (optional):** Bravery **Book title (optional):** The Little Old Lady Who Was Not Afraid of Anything

Play area	Monday	Tuesday	Wednesday	Thursday	Friday
Reading the Story	Read the story with the children helping with the lines and sounds. Hold up cue cards with the words printed on them.	Have the children wear a hat and gloves as the story is read. They can stand and act out the part of the story that is being read.	Repeat reading the story with all of the children wearing hats and gloves and acting out their parts. One child can lead the reading.	Repeat the previous day's activities.	Repeat reading the story for the last time. Have the children wear hats and gloves, or they may enjoy acting out the parts in the Dramatic Play: Theme Area.
Dramatic Play: Theme Area	Repeat the dramatization. Add a box at the end of the path that the old lady needs to go into to gather herbs.	Continue the dramatization of the story. Hang the clothing, and let the children take turns being the old lady.	Continue the dramatization of the story. Let the children direct as much as possible how they want to do the story. Facilitation should be minimal.	Continue the dramatization of the story. Let the children add their own improvisations.	Either repeat the dramatization with the children or have a final class production in which all of the children "read" the story.
Literacy Center	Use the flannel board pieces made at the Table Play area last week. Let the children tell the story and manipulate the figures.	Repeat the flannel board activity. Repeat the interactive story chart.	Play the Old Lady Memory game. Repeat the interactive story chart.	Play the Old Lady Memory game again. Repeat the interactive story chart.	Play the Old Lady Memory game again. Repeat the interactive story chart. Make up a new story.
Science and Math Center	Prior to class, cut small flaps into sheets of brown construction paper. Place seeds under the flaps to make a garden,	Repeat the study and planting of seeds. Use different seeds from the ones used the previous day.	Make pumpkin bread.	Make corn muffins.	Make granola muffins. Analyze the ingredients, and discuss where the different ingredients come from.
Art Area	Let the children use orange and black scraps of tissue paper to paste on a pumpkin-shaped piece of cardboard to make jack-o'-lanterns.	Use crumpled plastic wrap to dip into tempera paint mixed with water.	Let the children make sponge prints with watercolors or other washable paint. Then have them place a piece of paper over the prints and press.	Have one child lie down on newsprint, and have another child or you draw around the child. Let all of the children draw on the shape to make a scarecrow.	Repeat painting clothing. Make clay pictures.
Sensory Area	Discuss how spiderwebs are made. Make fake spiderwebs in the classroom. Make noisemakers out of Pringles cans. The gardening table remains.	Use face paints and a mirror to have the children paint their own faces or for you to paint their faces. The gardening table remains.	Repeat the face painting. Show the children how to make hand shadow puppets in the box at the end of the path.	Repeat the hand shadow puppets. In a feely box, place items for the children to reach in and identify.	Repeat the feely box. Add some new items. Have the children try out the noisemakers in the box to see if they sound different. The gardening table remains.
Motor Area	Wrap string around a platform swing (if available) or around a climber to represent a spiderweb.	Repeat the spiderweb on the swing or on the climber. Find a large, inflatable pumpkin for the children to roll at the scarecrow.	Repeat the previous day's activities. Let the children initiate the games and make up the rules.	Let the children choose what they want to do with the materials. Put orange chalk near the chalkboard, and show the children how to draw a giant pumpkin.	Repeat the previous day's activities.

Play-Based Curriculum Planning Sheet: Storybook Activities

Date: Week Two **Theme (optional):** Bravery **Book title (optional):** The Little Old Lady Who Was Not Afraid of Anything

Play area	Monday	Tuesday	Wednesday	Thursday	Friday
Floor Play	Play the Match the Clothing game. Repeat the puzzles, miniature dolls, pumpkins, and switch toys.	Make a Big and Small game board for the children to play. Repeat the puzzles, miniature dolls, pumpkins, and switch toys.	Have the children nail together three sets of wood strips to form three different size crosses on which clothing can be hung to make scarecrows.	Finish the scarecrows by letting the children make heads for them out of empty milk containers.	Play a Halloween board game.
Table Play	Make orange playdough. Let the children roll it out, make shapes with it, and so forth.	Bring out the playdough made the previous day. Let the children experiment with the different Halloween cookie cutters.	Make scarecrows. Repeat playing with the playdough. Model making clothing out of playdough.	Draw faces on paper plates. Make the colored plates into puzzles.	Repeat making puzzles. Cut out shapes in the Jell-O Jigglers with cookie cutters.
Outdoor Play	Take gardening tools outside to the sandbox. Let the children plant seeds in the garden. Free play.	Repeat gardening in the sandbox. Dress a broomstick as a scarecrow to place near the sandbox. Free play.	Play Old Lady Says. Let the children take turns being the old lady. Free play.	Take a box of clothing outside, and let the children dress up and pretend to be scarecrows. Play Scarecrow Says. Free play.	Play the Broom Ball game. Free play.
Snack	Oral motor: Make sounds, such as the wind blowing. Snack: Orange juice Popsicles and water	Oral motor: Pretend to make a milkshake in your mouth. Snack: Milkshakes	Oral motor: Repeat the previous day's "mouthwash" movements. Snack: Pumpkin bread and milk	Oral Motor: Make jack-o'-lantern faces. Snack: Corn muffins and orange juice	Oral motor: Repeat jack-o'-lantern faces. Snack: Granola muffins and milk
Books and Music					
Software					

TPBA Play-Based TPBI TPBC

VOCABULARY

Labels	Clay	Gloves	Pants
	Corn	Hands	Path
	Cottage	Hat	Pumpkin
	Crows	Hay	Scarecrow
	Fingers	Herbs	Seeds
	Flowers	House	Shirt
	Foot	Idea	Shoes
	Forest	Lady	Spices
	Garden	Pairs	Tomatoes
Action Words	Bang	Nod	Sniff
	Boo	Pick	Squeeze
	Brighten	Paste	Stop
	Catch your breath	Plant	Walk
	Clap	Push	Whisper
	Clomp	Run	Whistle
	Cut	Shake	Wiggle
	Go	Shine	
	Knock	Smell	
Descriptors	Afraid	Inside	Scared
	Anxious	Large, larger, largest	Scary
	Bad	Last	Sliver
	Behind	Light	Slow, slower, slowest
	Black	Long	Small, smaller, smallest
	Dry	Loud, louder, loudest	Soft
	Far	Mad	Unhappy
	Fast, faster, fastest	Mean	Wet
	Frightened	Noisier	White
	Good	Old	Windy
	Happy	Orange	Worried
	Hard, harder	Quiet	
	Heavy	Sad	

MATERIALS

Toys and Equipment

- Balls
- Battery-operated pumpkin toys or other Halloween switch toys (a witch can be the old lady)
- Blocks of different types
- Board games
- Broom
- Easel
- Flannel board
- Hammers
- Instruments (drums, tambourine, sticks, etc.)
- Koosh balls
- Legos
- Miniature characters and dolls clothing
- Miniature scarecrow, witch (for old lady), and pumpkin
- Musical instruments
- Platform swing
- Playdough or Play-Doh
- Puppets
- Puzzles of body parts, clothing, pumpkins, and so forth
- Rubber stamps (letters, shapes, numbers, pumpkins)
- Sand and water tables
- Sandbox or wading pool
- Small toys (e.g., people) for miniature scenario
- Stamp pads
- Tape recorder or record player

Supplies

- Basket
- Beans
- Brayer or rolling pin
- Bread pans
- Broomstick
- Cardboard
- Catalogs with pictures of clothing
- Clay
- Clothesline
- Clothespins
- Colander
- Construction paper
- Doll clothes and different sizes of clothing
- Empty milk containers (different sizes)
- Fabric or wallpaper samples
- Face paints
- Fall leaves
- Filmy scarves
- Flannel board pieces of a person and clothing
- Flashlights
- Gardening tools
- Gloves (children can bring in a pair from home, too)
- Glue
- Gray wig (if possible)
- Halloween spiderwebbing
- Herbs (or grass and weeds)
- Indian corn
- Inflatable pumpkin
- Large box into which children can crawl
- Magnifying glasses
- Measuring tapes
- Mixing bowls
- Mirrors
- Moon (a sliver) to hang from the ceiling
- Muffin pans
- Nails
- Newsprint and newspapers
- Oak tagboard
- Old clothes (to paint and to make a scarecrow)
- Old lady clothes (e.g., apron, hat, basket)
- Orange and black tissue paper
- Orange chalk
- Packages of flower and vegetable seeds
- Paint
- Pants
- Paper bags for paper bag scarecrows
- Paper muffin cups
- Paper plates (in different colors)
- Pencil erasers
- Pictures from the story
- Plastic baggies
- Plastic needles (large)
- Plastic pumpkins
- Plastic tubs
- Plastic wrap
- Popsicle sticks
- Poster board
- Pringles cans
- Protective cover sheets
- Pumpkin cookie cutters
- Pumpkin head

Pumpkin to carve
Rubber bands
Rulers (inch or centimeter)
Safety pins
Scales or balance
Shirt
Shoes (e.g., work boots, hiking boots)
Socks
Sponges
Spoons
Straw
Straws
Streamers
String
Styrofoam meat trays
Tape of the story being read
Tempera paints
Three-ring binders
Toaster oven (or access to oven)
Toothbrushes
Top hats (children can bring a hat from home, too)
Tree branches in coffee cans
Velcro or flannel
Washcloths
Waxed paper
White felt
Wood strips

Food

Apple juice
Baking powder
Baking soda
Basil
Canned pumpkin
Cinnamon
Cinnamon rice cakes
Cloves (ground)
Cooking spray
Crackers (sesame and wheat)
Cream cheese
Creamed corn
Eggs
Flour (white and whole wheat)
Ginger
Granola
Herb cracker spreads
Herbs
Honey
Ice cream
Jell-O Jigglers
Juice
Lemonade
Milk
Nuts
Oil
Orange juice
Orange Kool-Aid
Oregano
Pumpkin seeds
Salt
Shortening
Spices
Sugar
Vanilla
Yellow cornmeal

*See the sample ClickArt® at the end of the *Teacher's Guide*.

READING THE STORY

You can dress up like the old lady as you read the story, or another team member can act out the story as it is read. This will heighten the children's interest and help to hold their attention.

WEEK 1

Day 1 This story is fun to read because the children can become so involved. On the first day, hide all of the props behind you, and bring them out one by one as they appear in the story. Clomp, clomp the heavy shoes; then wiggle, wiggle a pair of pants; and so forth.

Day 2 Read the story. Repeat the actions from the previous day with the props, but have an extra set to hand to one of the children as the part of the story in which that prop appears is read. Let the child with the prop act out the noises and actions with you. As each new prop is added, each of the previous children will get to play their part again, or the props can be passed to another child.

Day 3 Read the story. You can hand out two sets of props to the children so that now two children get a pair of shoes, another two children get the pants, and so forth. Have the children who are assisting stand or sit by you so that you can help them to concentrate on their roles.

Day 4 Repeat reading the story with enough sets of props that each child gets a prop. (If shoes and gloves are divided, the children who have them will need to work together to go "clomp, clomp" and "clap, clap"). You can begin to omit the sound or action to see if the children can fill in the blank. Children who tend to play with the props and not listen may need assistance.

Day 5 Before reading and telling the story again, let one or two children who made a book in the Literacy Center share their books with the group. Use a flannel board to tell the story. Let the children assist in predicting and participating in putting up the flannel pieces.

WEEK 2

Day 1 Read the story with the children each helping with the lines and sounds. Hold up cue cards with the words printed on them (e.g., "CLOMP, CLOMP!"). The children will remember the words and be able to "read" them. Point to each word as it is read.

Day 2 Have each child wear a hat and gloves. As the story is read, they can stand and act out that part of the story (e.g., stomping their feet, wiggling their bottoms, shaking their shoulders, clapping their hands, nodding their heads, shouting "BOO!").

Day 3 Repeat reading the story with all of the children wearing hats and gloves and acting out their parts. Have one child lead the "reading."

Day 4 Repeat reading the story with all of the children wearing hats and gloves and acting out their parts. Have a different child lead the "reading." You can be the pumpkin head.

Day 5 Repeat reading the story for the last time with all of the children wearing hats and gloves, or you may want to do the final reading in the Dramatic Play: Theme Area, with the children acting out the parts. (See Dramatic Play: Theme Area, Week 2, Day 5.)

Sensorimotor Level

1. Involve children at the sensorimotor level in the movement of objects after observing their peers.
2. Emphasize the sounds and actions of the pieces of clothing (e.g., clomp, wiggle, shake).
3. Prompt the movements, with facilitation, for the children at this level with visual impairments or for those who cannot initiate.
4. Encourage sound production and imitation of sounds and words in these children.
5. If these children can label "hat" or any other part in the pictures, let them participate by labeling the object for the group.

Functional Level

1. Children at this level will imitate you without much prompting. Exaggerate the voice of the little old lady to draw attention to her words.
2. Emphasize to these children the sounds and actions plus the character of the little old lady. Point out the little old lady's props (e.g., apron, basket, hat).
3. Involve children at this level as models in acting out and saying key words.
4. Point to the word as you read the key phrases to these children.
5. Have these children help to turn the pages.
6. Encourage these children to repeat key words and phrases. In order to increase sentence length, add one more word from the story to whatever length of phrase the child says spontaneously. For example, if the child

points to the shoes and says, "CLOMP! CLOMP!" you can add, "Shoes CLOMP! CLOMP!" For children capable of using longer phrases, you may model the whole phrase, "Two shoes go CLOMP, CLOMP!"

Symbolic Level

1. Involve the children at the symbolic level in the telling of the story as well as the actions and key words. They will be able to repeat the little old lady's comments to the clothing.
2. Let these children help predict what the little old lady will meet next.
3. These children can be the main models for the other children in acting out the roles in the story.
4. Have these children identify key words in print and help you "read" the story.
5. These children can choose the correct cue card and hold it up after several days of seeing the cards matched to the story. You may help these children match configuration, length of word, or first-letter sounds to select the correct card.

DRAMATIC PLAY: THEME AREA

The house and theme areas are combined in this story, with a path leading through a "forest." The forest is composed of tree branches in coffee cans and streamers hanging from the ceiling. A sliver of a moon can also be hung from the ceiling. Later in the first week, a box large enough for the children to crawl into can be added at the end of the path for the old lady to crawl into to gather her seeds and herbs. The old lady will need a basket to carry her seeds and herbs. If this module follows the module based on *Picking Apples & Pumpkins,* you can use the pumpkins and other creations for this module as well.

WEEK 1

Day 1

You will first need to dramatize the story. The sequence of actions to be portrayed includes the following:

1. The old lady walks down the path and gathers herbs, spices, nuts, and seeds.
2. The old lady encounters the pieces of clothing and the pumpkin head.
3. The old lady runs home and tells the clothing that she is not afraid.

The action sequence will be enhanced or diminished depending on the children who choose to be involved. Create a script to go along with the sequence. Act out the script with the sequence.

The pieces of clothing can be incorporated in one of several ways. They can be hung by string from the ceiling so that they dangle on the way down the path; they can be laid on the path, and someone can shake them when the old woman approaches; they can be draped over a stick (except for the shoes) and stuck into the path as the old woman passes; or the children can wear the shoes, pants, and so forth and act out the parts. You may want to use a variety of methods because each supports development in different ways. For example, having the clothing hanging from the ceiling allows a child to go to that center and act out the story alone. Having a child wave the clothing on a stick encourages that child to learn the sequence of actions and props, an important skill for children at both the functional and symbolic levels. When individual children act out the roles of various pieces of clothing, more children can be involved in the story and peer cooperation is needed. For all of these reasons, a mixture of approaches may be beneficial.

After the demonstration, you can see who wants to be the old lady and who wants to help with the pieces of clothing. The children can then act it out with your prompting. On the first day, you may want to have individual children play the clothing parts, as observing their peers act out the sequence may aid their memory.

Day 2 Repeat having the children act out the story. You can now support the children in acting out the story, prompting the lines from the script you have created. The script is adapted to the level of the child playing the role of the old lady. Individual children may play clothing parts.

Day 3 Repeat having the children act out the story. Add herbs (grass and weeds will do) and nuts along the path for the old lady to gather.

Day 4 Continue with the dramatization and the script. Have the children take turns acting out the clothing parts so that they remember the sequence.

Day 5 Repeat the dramatization and the script. You may want to alter the path so that the little old lady goes down a winding path. You can do this by adding a rope or some tape to the path that the little old lady can follow.

WEEK 2

Day 1 Continue with the dramatization of the story. Add a box at the end of the path for the old lady to go into to get herbs and nuts. Put a flashlight in the box. Turn out the lights when she comes out of the box so that she can use her flashlight to walk home.

Day 2 Continue with the dramatization of the story. You may want to hang the clothing now, and let the children take turns being the old lady. This will let a child act out the whole sequence with very little facilitation. Other children can add scary noises (e.g., the wind blowing "whoooo" and the sound of leaves [use the noisemakers made the previous day in the Sensory Area, Week 2, Day 1]).

Day 3 Continue the dramatization of the story and script with the box, flashlight, and scary noises. Let the children direct as much as possible how they want to do the story. Facilitation should be minimal.

Day 4 Continue the dramatization of the story and script. Let the children add their own improvisations.

Day 5

Today you may want to repeat the dramatization with the children who select this center, or you may want a final class production in which all of the children "read" the story. Different children can be assigned the roles of the little old lady, shoes, and so forth. Have some children be in the audience as noisemakers, and act out the story as a class one more time.

Sensorimotor Level

1. Children at the sensorimotor level may be involved in making the sounds and actions of the clothing. Some may be able to label the shoes, shirt, and so forth.
2. Encourage these children to explore the characteristics of each of the props (e.g., smelling the herbs, clapping with gloves on).
3. Have these children label all props and actions with one to two words (e.g., "Lady walk").

Functional Level

1. Children at the functional level will enthusiastically stomp and shake. Work on increasing their memory of the sequence of actions. Let them tell you what is next. At this level, encourage a two- to three-step sequence. You can cue them by showing the next prop.
2. Label descriptors (e.g., "loud," "soft," "scary," "fast") for these children.
3. Encourage these children to use phrases and short sentences.
4. Point out the printed labels in the area (e.g., "old lady's house," "path"). Hold up cue cards as these children say the words so that they will begin to understand that words on paper can correspond with words that are said.

Symbolic Level

1. Let the children at the symbolic level help determine what is needed in the area and help set up.
2. As the story is first enacted, these children can act as models for the children at the other levels. Have these children plan the sequence.
3. Encourage the use of the script, although these children can improvise and add material.

4. Encourage the expression of emotions (e.g., worried, anxious, scared, frightened) with these children.
5. Let some of these children become the directors of the script and actions.
6. Use the cue cards to prompt the script with these children, and let these children use the cue cards with their peers.

LITERACY CENTER

WEEK 1

Have the tape and book available in this center for the children to listen to and "read." One idea is to have an extra copy of the book that can be dismantled and either laminated or put in sheet protectors and then into a three-ring binder. This will enable the children to turn the pages easily and to go back and forth in the book without worrying about tearing the pages. Having the book in a three-ring binder also enables children who have difficulty holding a book, looking at the pictures, or turning pages to more easily be able to "read" the story.

Day 1

Make labels for the Dramatic Play: Theme Area and the garden. Labels can include "old lady's house," "path," "forest," "shoes," "pants," "shirt," "hat," "gloves," "pumpkin," "garden," and "scarecrow." Label the children's footprints made in the Art Area with their names. Have the children write their own names or part of their names if they can. Some may want to try tracing their names.

Day 2

Make books of clothing. Have the children cut out pictures of clothing from catalogs and paste them onto pieces of paper (a half sheet of regular typing paper or a 4″ × 5″ piece of construction paper is a good size). Label the clothing on each page, allowing each child to write as much as he or she can.

Day 3

Finish the books the children began the previous day. They can now make a cover (draw a person or something else of their choice), staple all of the pages and the cover together, and make up a title to write on the front. These may also be laminated and hole-punched and held together in a three-ring binder.

At the literacy table, place out several different spices and herbs. Pick ones that would be found in foods the children eat, such as oregano, cinnamon, basil, and ginger. Discuss why the old lady is looking for herbs, spices, nuts, and seeds and where they are found. Have the children smell each of the spices and describe it. Descriptions can be simple (e.g., "good," "bad") or more descriptive (e.g., "like hay"). Write down the name of each spice on a small piece of paper and tape the label to the bottle. You may also want to write down on a piece of paper the words or phrases the children use to describe each one.

Day 4

Let the children draw or find pictures of things that make them scared. Label each picture using the children's words. Look at the pictures in *The Little Old Lady Who Was Not Afraid of Anything*. Talk about whether the little old lady was really scared and what she did when she got scared. Discuss what the children can do if they get scared. Use an interactive storyboard with a section from the last two pages in the book. On a large piece of poster board, write the words from the last two pages of the storybook to make an interactive storyboard. Under each line of the story, tape an extra strip of poster board to make a pocket that goes all the way across the board. Make a second set of sentences that matches the set on the board. Each line should be on a separate piece of cardboard and should fit into the pocket under the appropriate matching line. (As an alternative to the strips under each line on the chart, Velcro tabs or magnetic tabs can be placed above each word on the chart and on the back of the cards.) Make a third set of cards that match the first and last words of each line so that the word, when placed in the pocket, will match and cover the word space above it. Make a fourth set of poster board strips to match the ones you have just completed, only leave them blank. This set of cards can now be used with the children to let them see the familiar words from the story. The children can also use this interactive story chart to play games (e.g., when the words or sentences are covered with the blank cards, the children can try to find and place the appropriate words in the slot). Such interactive boards are a great way to let children experiment with matching, memory for words and sequences, sound–letter association, configuration matching, and creative or humorous alterations in the story.

Day 5 Have the children dictate a story about something that is scary. You may want to use the model of the little old lady. For example, you may start the children off by saying, "A little boy went for a walk in the park when behind him he heard a. . . ." This is a fun small-group activity, as each child can contribute ideas in building the story. Repeat the interactive storyboard.

WEEK 2

Day 1 Use the flannel board pieces made at the Table Play area the previous week. Let the children tell the story and manipulate the pieces by themselves. Make some pieces with the key words on them, such as "CLAP, CLAP!" (These can be written on white felt or on oaktag with a piece of Velcro attached.) Accuracy in telling the story is not the goal for most of the children; sequencing ideas, relating words and objects, and having fun with the characters are the goals. Repeat the interactive story chart.

Day 2 Repeat the flannel board activity. If a particular child is interested, you can write down the child's words as he or she tells the story. Seeing your words in print is always exciting! Repeat the interactive story chart.

Day 3 Play the Old Lady Memory game. Write the sets of words from the story (e.g., "CLOMP, CLOMP!") on small paper pumpkins (one word on each pumpkin). Have the children who are able copy the word after you write the first word in the set (e.g., you write "SHAKE" on one pumpkin, the child copies, traces, connects the dots to make "SHAKE" on another pumpkin). Pictures of clothing can also be used instead of words. After this process is complete for all of the sets of words (or pictures of clothing) in the story ("CLOMP, CLOMP"; "WIGGLE, WIGGLE"; "SHAKE, SHAKE"; "CLAP, CLAP"; "NOD, NOD"; "BOO, BOO"), the pumpkins are mixed up and turned over to play the game of memory. Each player tries to remember where the matching word is and gets to keep the set if the match is correct. The number of sets turned over can be adjusted to meet the level of children playing the game. (If possible, laminate the pumpkins for future play.) Repeat the interactive story chart.

Day 4 Play the Old Lady Memory game again. If more challenge is needed, more words and/or pictures from the story can be added. Repeat the interactive story chart.

Day 5 Play the Old Lady Memory game again. Repeat the interactive story chart. Use the words on the pumpkins to make up a new story. Ask the children what else could go CLOMP, CLOMP! After coming up with the variation or new story, you can write the story down to be posted on the wall. This is a good activity for a group of children. What they come up with does not have to be logical. Engaging the imagination and elucidating a story sequence is what is desired.

Sensorimotor Level

1. Marking on paper with an orange marker (like a pumpkin) will be appropriate for children at the sensorimotor level who choose to come to this center.
2. These children may also enjoy looking at magazines, and you can point out and label pictures.
3. The children at the symbolic level may enjoy "reading" their books to the children at the sensorimotor level.
4. Children at this level may be able to use the story in the three-ring binder more easily than the real book, and the binder, which opens out flat, can be used by these children without adult assistance when they just want to look at the pictures.

Functional Level

1. Let children at the functional level experiment with writing, even if their efforts do not resemble real letters.
2. Let these children use stamp pads with letters, shapes, and numbers. A pumpkin stamp would be fun for them.

3. These children will also enjoy experimenting with the flannel board characters. You may want to facilitate their use of key words and the memory of the sequence within the story by giving clues (e.g., pointing to the top of your head for the hat).
4. These children can try to cut out pictures (some will need assistance) and paste them down. Label their pictures with written words so that they begin to associate print with concepts.

Symbolic Level

1. Activities at this center are particularly relevant for children at the symbolic level. Encourage them to write letters and words as they are able.
2. Encourage dictation of complete sentences by these children.
3. Incorporate into this center key vocabulary concepts, particularly those related to emotions (e.g., anxious, frightened, scared), for these children.
4. Promote creative thought and accept creative spelling if these children begin to write on their own.

SCIENCE AND MATH CENTER

WEEK 1

Day 1

Study different herbs and spices under a magnifying glass. Tape or paste samples onto a piece of paper, or have the children place samples into a small plastic baggie, and then tape the baggie to a sheet of stiff paper. Help the children label each sample. Describe how the herbs and spices smell and what kind of food would taste good with that herb or spice. If possible, let them taste something that has the spice in it. Display the mounted samples in a professional manner in this center.

Day 2

Help the children to carve a pumpkin on which a face was drawn in the Art Area the previous day. Let the children take turns scooping out the insides with a spoon, and then show them how to pull the seeds out with their fingers and place them in a colander. When the pumpkin is cleaned out and the insides discarded, have the children wash the seeds in the colander under running water. They can then spread the seeds out on a tray to be baked later and served for a snack.

Measure the footprints that were made in the Art Area on Day 1 using a ruler or a piece of string to compare lengths. See whether the children can determine whose feet are the largest or longest, whose are the smallest or shortest, and whose are the same size.

Day 3

Have the children take off one shoe each. Let them line them up next to one another and determine which is the largest, smallest, and so forth. Using a cloth measuring tape, let the children measure the length of each other's pants or skirts. Write down the lengths, and find the smallest and largest numbers. Which pants or skirts were the longest? Which were the shortest?

Day 4

Weigh a pair of the adult's shoes and then a pair of the children's shoes. Compare the weights. Which weighs more? Which weighs less? Measure them. Which is the longest? Which is the shortest? Which ones are big, bigger, and biggest?

Day 5

Continue to measure and weigh the children's shoes and make comparisons. Add concepts, such as *first* and *last* (e.g., "Which one did we measure *first* or measure *last*?").

Day 1

WEEK 2

Prior to class, take sheets of brown construction paper, and cut small flaps into the paper in straight rows. Tape these onto the floor so the rows of flaps line up to make long rows. This "plot of land" will become the old lady's garden. Let the children in this center sort packages of seeds into two groups: vegetables and flowers. (Garden shops will usually give you old seeds.) Remove a few of the seeds from each package, and let the children study them under a magnifying glass. (Tear off the bottom of the package rather than the top. The package will be used later.) Discuss with the children which seeds are the largest and which ones are the smallest. Let the children decide where to plant the flowers and vegetables in the garden. Let them place a seed or two under each flap. Show the children how to place a Popsicle stick in a chunk of Play-Doh, put the seed package on top, and then stick the clay on the flaps under which the seeds are planted.

Day 2

Repeat the study and planting of seeds. Use different seeds from the ones used the previous day.

Day 3

For the next 3 days, the children may make snacks in this center. This will allow them repeated practice in measuring and following the sequence of a recipe.

Make pumpkin bread this day. Let the children mix all of ingredients, set the oven temperature, and set the timer for baking. Make a picture chart for the children to follow.

PUMPKIN BREAD

1¾ cups of all-purpose flour
¼ teaspoon of double-acting baking powder
1 teaspoon of baking soda
1 teaspoon of salt
½ teaspoon of cinnamon
¼ teaspoon of ground cloves
1⅓ cups of sugar
⅓ cup of shortening
2 eggs
1 cup of cooked or canned pumpkin
⅓ cup of water or milk
½ teaspoon of vanilla
½ cup of raisins, optional

In a large bowl, sift together the flour, baking powder, baking soda, cinnamon, and ground cloves. Then, in another large bowl, beat the sugar, shortening, salt, and eggs until fluffy. Add the pumpkin to the sugar mixture. Do not over beat between each addition. Now add the sifted dry ingredients along with the water or milk and vanilla to the sugar mixture in three additions. You may fold in the raisins at this point, if desired. Let a child set the oven for 350 degrees to preheat it. Let another child grease a bread pan with cooking spray or oil wiped around the pan with a paper towel. Pour the batter into the bread pan and bake for 1 hour or until done.

The bread can then be cooled and saved for today's snack.

Day 4 Make corn muffins. Let the children measure and mix the ingredients, set the oven temperature, and set the timer for baking the muffins. Make a picture chart for the children to follow.

CORN MUFFINS

1 cup of whole wheat flour
1 cup of all-purpose flour (or if whole wheat flour is unavailable, use 2 cups of all-purpose flour)
2 cups of yellow cornmeal
2 tablespoons of baking powder
1½ teaspoons of salt
½ cup of sugar *or* honey
2 cups of milk
2 eggs
½ cup of oil

Have a child set the oven at 400 degrees to preheat it. Let the children stir together the flour, cornmeal, baking powder, salt, and sugar. In another bowl, let them thoroughly mix the milk, eggs, and oil together. Pour this mixture into the dry ingredients. Stir until just moistened. Let the batter sit for 5 minutes, while the children are preparing the muffin pans by inserting the paper liners. Give the children small measuring cups to fill each of the muffin cups two thirds full. Bake the muffins for 15–20 minutes or until done. Makes up to 24 muffins (depending on how full the children fill the cups and how much they spill).

Day 5 Make granola muffins. Analyze all of the ingredients, and discuss which ingredients come from which types of plants or animals (show the children various pictures of wheat, a chicken, grapes, oats, and so forth). Let the children try to figure out which of the ingredients originated from each of the items in the pictures.

GRANOLA MUFFINS

1½ cups of whole wheat flour
1½ cups of unbleached all-purpose flour
1½ tablespoons of baking powder
¾ teaspoon of salt
½ cup of butter or margarine
2 cups of granola
2 eggs
1 cup of milk
4 teaspoons of cinnamon

Preheat the oven to 400 degrees. Blend the flour, baking powder, and salt in a large mixing bowl. Using an electric mixer, food processor, or pastry blender, cut the butter or margarine into the flour mixture until it resembles course cornmeal. Stir together the flour mixture and granola. In another bowl, mix the eggs and milk together well. Add this mixture to the dry ingredients. Stir until just moistened. Fill paper-lined muffin pans two thirds full. Bake for 20 minutes or until golden brown. Makes 24 muffins.

Sensorimotor Level

1. Children at the sensorimotor level can try to smell the spices. They may want to touch the spices as well, so be sure that children who have a tendency to mouth objects do not have access to hot spices. (Also be sure to find out whether any of the children are allergic to any of the spices and so forth.)
2. These children may be able to take the seeds and pulp out of the pumpkin. Let them run the water over the material in the colander.
3. When the other children are weighing and measuring shoes, these children can label the "shoe" and "foot," and you can demonstrate putting on the shoes and assist the children in taking off and putting on their shoes. Let peers at the symbolic level measure the shoes for these children. (Children at the functional level may also pretend to measure.)
4. Label the pictures on the packages of seeds as "flower," "tomato," and so forth for these children. Although the children at this level may not understand *planting* the seeds, they may be able to hide the seeds in the paper pockets.
5. For all of the cooking activities, these children can help dump in the ingredients and stir them into the mixture.

Functional Level

1. The children at the functional level may like looking at the spices with magnifying glasses and pouring some of them into plastic bags. You can emphasize the words "smell," "like," "good," "bad," and so forth.
2. Although you will need to guide these children, you should encourage them to help carve the pumpkin with a safety pumpkin knife as it requires the children to push against resistance, use eye–hand coordination, and relate the lines on the pumpkin to a face.
3. Although these children will not understand measurement, they should be encouraged to compare the shoes and choose the "big one," the "small one," the "heavy one," and so forth. The comparison of two objects is the goal as well as the identification of an appropriate description.
4. Have these children count the shoes and label colors.
5. Encourage children at this level to follow a sequence of steps in planting the seeds: a) take the seed out of the package, b) place the seed under a flap, c) and close the flap; and a) stick the Popsicle stick in the Play-Doh, b) place the seed wrapper on the stick, and c) place the stick in the garden. Label the seeds, pictures on the packages, actions, and sizes.
6. Encourage the children at this level to look at the picture charts for the recipes. Relate the pictures to the next action in the sequence. Let the children find the objects in the picture chart, if possible. Discuss what a

particular child is doing as he or she is pouring, stirring, and so forth, and then let the child look at the chart to determine what should happen next.

Symbolic Level

1. Let the children at the symbolic level analyze the different shapes, sizes, and smells of the spices and herbs. Let the children attempt to copy or trace the labels on the pictures.
2. Let these children help poke holes with the needle on the lines of the face drawn on the pumpkin. They can be involved in all aspects of the process of cutting and emptying the pumpkin. They may want to demonstrate or assist their peers in various aspects of the process.
3. Children at this level can begin to make comparisons among three or more objects when weighing and measuring. Encourage these children to sequence, measure, and label the shoes with various labels, such as the "biggest," the "first," the "last," the "heaviest," the "lightest," and other comparative and ordinal terms.
4. Assist these children in using one-to-one correspondence with counting the marks on the measuring tools and the corresponding numbers. Encourage number identification.
5. Children at this level will enjoy planting the garden and will be able to understand that it is a pretend garden. Encourage the discrimination of characteristics among the different seeds and the classification of flowers, vegetables, and fruits. Discuss the planting, growing, weeding, and picking process.
6. For all of the recipes, encourage these children to measure the ingredients and follow the sequence as indicated on the chart. Discuss the "dry" and "wet" ingredients, and encourage the children to describe what they are doing and predict what will be needed next.

ART AREA

WEEK 1

Day 1

Roll out a long strip of newsprint. You may want to draw a yellow (or other light color) line that curves and loops down the path for the children to follow. Have the children step in a pan of paint in their bare feet and walk down the path. Have them step into a pan of water at the end, wash their feet, and dry them. Label each child's footprints with his or her name. This "foot mural" can be taped down to the floor to become the path on which the old lady walks.

Let the children draw the face on the pumpkin. Look at the picture of the pumpkin in the book, and let the children decide whether they want to make the face similar to the one in the story or design their own face. You can assist the children in making the face. The children can then use large, plastic needles to poke holes in the pumpkin along the lines forming the face. This activity requires eye–hand coordination and the use of some pressure, which is good for building muscle tone and strength in the fingers.

Put out an easel with paints of different colors. Some children may prefer to paint a picture of a pumpkin or other item from the story.

Day 2

Bring in *old,* light-colored clothing, and let the children paint designs on them. They may use a variety of tools (e.g., pencil erasers dipped in paint to make polka dots, paintbrushes, sponges, toothbrushes) to make their designs.

Day 3

Hang a set of clothing (the pieces named in the story) with clothespins on a clothesline (similar to the picture on the third page of the storybook) against one wall. Tape a long piece of art paper on the wall underneath the clothing. Have the students start painting a mural with bright colored poster paints. Let them try to match the colors and shapes of the clothing that is hanging right above the mural. Each child can choose what he or she wants to paint. It is fine if there are five children who want to paint pants on the mural. It is also fine if none of the children's efforts resemble the actual clothing.

Day 4

Let those children who are interested continue working on the mural. Use Magic Markers to add

buttons, zippers, and other details to the mural. Set an actual pumpkin or jack-o'-lantern cut like the face in the story next to the easel for children to look at and attempt to paint a pumpkin or other picture. Setting out orange and black paint may be a motivator to try to paint a pumpkin. You can point out the characteristics of the pumpkin, such as shape, eyes, nose, and mouth. When the child is finished painting, label the parts of the picture as the child describes it. This will assist parents in communicating with their children about the piece of art and will link the written label to the picture for the child.

Day 5 Continue painting on the mural and on the easels. Cut sponges into the shapes of a person, a top hat, a glove, pants, and/or a shirt, and let the children experiment with making prints from the sponges dipped in paint on waxed paper or construction paper. Some children may want to cut out the painted clothing. You can draw tabs on the clothing and show the children how to fold the tabs over the person to make a paper doll with clothing. (If paper dolls are made, then use heavier paper, oak tagboard, or cardboard for the person and construction paper for the clothing.)

WEEK 2

Day 1 Let the children cut orange and black scraps of tissue paper into small pieces (or shapes) and paste the orange pieces on a pumpkin-shaped piece of cardboard or a large paper plate to make jack-o'-lanterns. Then with the small black pieces, the children can paste on the eyes, nose, and mouth.

Day 2 Use crumpled plastic wrap to dip into tempera paint mixed with water. When pressed against another piece of paper or fabric, the crumpled plastic wrap will leave interesting patterns. Let the children make "wrinkled shirts" or "pants" on the paper. Continue to make tissue paper pumpkins. The children may want to paint over their creation with a mixture of white glue and water to make it appear shiny.

Day 3 Let the children make sponge prints on the tabletops (only if the tops are Formica or another washable surface) with watercolors or other washable paint. Place a piece of white paper on top of their art and have them press down on the paper. They may also use a brayer or a rolling pin to roll over the paper. Then let them carefully lift their paper and look at the print on the other side. When the print is dry, a frame can be made from multicolored, precut construction paper strips glued to the edges. Let the children figure out which strips match the length or width of the paper. These framed designs may be hung around the room.

Day 4 Let one child (or more if the children want) lie down on newsprint, and have another child or you draw around the child. The children who have chosen to come to this area can then draw a face, pants, shirt, hat, and gloves. Glue on some straw, and cut out the image. Voilà! A scarecrow. Place on a wall either inside the classroom or outside in the hall.

Day 5 Repeat painting clothing. Make clay pictures. Use rectangular Styrofoam meat trays, and let the children work together. Let them design a piece of art by taking small pieces of clay in different fall colors and pushing them down on the trays in different patterns. Allow the clay pictures to dry, and then hang them on the walls.

Sensorimotor Level

1. The children at the sensorimotor level may be fascinated by stepping in the paint (or having their foot placed in the paint) and seeing the mark left by their foot. This is a good way to let them see cause and effect using their own body. Point out the *foot*print and whose footprint it is. Let the children help wash and dry their own feet.
2. These children may be able to paint on the easel or the mural more easily with a sponge paintbrush that you or a peer has dipped in the paint. Sitting in a chair may also help to stabilize these children. If you are concerned about the mess, the child may use plain water or watercolor paints. Even with clear water, the children will still be able to see the effect of the brush on the paper before the water dries.
3. Let these children use the clothing-shaped sponges. Add a piece of dowel that is glued to the top of the sponge to make a handle so that these children can manipulate the sponge more easily. Add dowels to the sponges used on the tabletop as well.
4. These children can help tear the tissue paper scraps.
5. Dipping the plastic wrap in paint and making marks on the paper will show these children cause and effect. If these children are unable to manipulate the plastic wrap to dip and paint, then let them squeeze and release the plastic wrap to watch its movement.
6. If the children at this level do not mouth the clay, they can squeeze and place small pieces of clay on the Styrofoam trays in imitation of their peers. Label the body parts (e.g., "hands," "fingers"), actions (e.g., "squeeze," "push"), and materials (e.g., "clay," "playdough").

Functional Level

1. Children at the functional level will appreciate the effect of painting with their feet. Let them watch and imitate their peers through the sequence of actions.
2. Let these children attempt to use the plastic needle to poke holes in the pumpkins (ideally on the line of the pumpkin's face!).
3. Let these children experiment with using different tools to see the different marks made by the various tools on the clothing.

4. You may want to draw an outline of a shirt, pants, and so forth on the paper under the clothesline so that these children can have an idea of what is being painted. You can encourage these children to pick colors that match the colors of the clothing hanging above the painting.
5. These children may not be able to understand painting a picture of a pumpkin, but they will enjoy painting with the orange and black paint. You may want to pair these children with a peer so that they can paint a picture with a partner. If paired with children at the symbolic level, then they may be able to learn from their partners, as the partners point out the face parts and how to paint them.
6. Encourage children at this level (who may need a sponge with a dowel attached) to relate the sponge shape to the appropriate piece of clothing. You may request a certain shape or help them label each piece of clothing as the sponge is pressed to the paper.
7. Help these children to make a pumpkin by gluing the orange tissue paper first on the pumpkin-shaped cardboard or paper plate. Do not be surprised if the result does not resemble a pumpkin. Emphasize completing a sequence: a) put glue on the paper plate, b) pick out a piece of tissue paper, and c) push the paper down on the glue.
8. Show these children how to squeeze the plastic wrap, dip it in the paint, and press it on paper or cloth.
9. These children may enjoy lying on the floor to have a peer draw around them. Encourage them to add facial parts and clothing.
10. Making clay pictures, which requires no structure, will be fun for these children. Draw their names in the clay with a sharp utensil so that each child can begin to recognize his or her name.

Symbolic Level

1. Let the children at this level draw a line on the paper on which to make a path to walk. Suggest different ways or let them determine creative ways to paint with their feet (e.g., on their toes, backward, sideways).
2. These children will be able to select and draw a face on the pumpkin. Encourage them to make the facial parts large enough to fill the pumpkin.
3. When painting on clothing, discuss pattern and design with these children. Let them make a pattern with different tools and then try to repeat the pattern.
4. Children at this level will enjoy studying the model of the clothing or the pumpkin and then attempting to draw the shirt, pumpkin, and so forth. Although the result may not look like the model, these children will understand that they are trying to make a picture to represent something in particular. They can also be encouraged to match colors.
5. Making sponge paintings with the clothing-shaped sponges will be fun for these children. They can experiment with sequencing the sponges to make a body.

6. Let these children experiment with making different faces with the tissue paper before gluing down the black pieces.
7. These children will enjoy making patterns with the plastic wrap and the sponge prints on the tabletop. Help the children to see the relationship between the pattern on the original piece and the pattern on the final piece.
8. The children at this level can determine where and how to draw the facial features and clothing. They can assist other children to participate in this activity.

SENSORY AREA

A variety of sensory experiences can be incorporated into this module. Some of the activities extend over several days so that the children can experiment, whereas others are offered only once to add an element of surprise.

WEEK 1

Day 1 Place dirt in the sand and water table to simulate the old lady's garden. Place gardening tools in the table and a plastic baggie with three different beans and pumpkin seeds in it for planting. The children can pretend to plant seeds or "cultivate" the soil.

Day 2 Add the garden labels (glued on Popsicle sticks so that they can be stuck in the dirt) made in the Literacy Center. Bring in old clothes to make a scarecrow. Have the children stuff the clothes with newspapers. Add the paper bag head made at the Table Play area. The children can seat the scarecrow in a chair by the dirt table garden.

Day 3 The children can try to dig up and find the seeds they planted, placing them in a plastic bag as they count them, and then start over on the planting process. Shell Indian corn into a basket. This requires effort by the children to push the kernels off into the container. This activity, which is good for children who need to increase hand strength and tone, also works on fine motor coordination.

At the Literacy Center, place a basket with bottles of different spices in it. The children can smell the spices and decide whether they like the smell and describe what it smells like (see the Literacy Center for the literacy aspect of this project).

Day 4 Add a large box to the end of the path. When the old lady comes to the box on the path, she can crawl into the box and find seeds, herbs, nuts, and so forth to put into her basket. Have a flashlight in her basket or in the box to help her look for the materials. This is an activity that children who like to crawl into small places will enjoy. Having some real herbs or grasses that have a smell will add an olfactory aspect to the experience. Placing them in the box will confine the odor and, therefore, strengthen the smell. Place the box at the end of the path so that the children who want to explore it without being involved in the dramatic play can do so. Continue the corn shelling activity.

Day 5 Repeat the previous day's activities.

WEEK 2

Day 1 Discuss how spiderwebs are made in the forest. Show the children pictures of spiderwebs. Using spiderwebbing, have the children pull it apart and tape it across the window in the room or across the tree branches on the path. If available, add little plastic spiders.

Make noisemakers out of potato chip cans (Pringles cans are good). Have the children crush fall leaves with their fingers and hands and put them in the can. If the pieces are small enough, then the children can put them through a funnel (ones made from the end of a plastic bleach bottle have wide openings and a handle). They can make some shakers with leaves, some with corn, and some with beans or seeds to compare the sounds. Have each child decorate and label the outside of his or her shaker and write his or her name on the can. The gardening table remains. By now this area should not need much facilitation.

Day 2 Use face paints and a mirror for children to paint their own faces or to have you paint their faces for them. They can have a jack-o'-lantern face or a scarecrow face. Many children will not want an adult to put things on their faces, but they will happily mess around with putting things on their own faces. It is not important whether the face really looks like a jack-o'-lantern. The goal is for the children to experiment with the texture of paint and, if appropriate, to make an effort at making themselves look like something else. The gardening table remains.

Day 3 Repeat the face painting. Some children may not have gotten to this area or may have just worked up the courage to try it. Others may want to do it again! Show the children how to make hand shadow puppets with the flashlight on the inside of the box at the end of the path. You can encourage cooperation by having one child hold the flashlight while the other one moves his or her hands. The gardening table remains.

Day 4 Repeat the hand shadow puppets. In a feely box, place items for the children to reach in and identify. The items can be from the story (e.g., glove, hat, small pumpkin, shoe). The gardening table remains.

Day 5 Repeat the feely box. Add some new items as well, such as pieces of corn, beans, and pumpkin seeds. Have the children try out the noisemakers in the box to see if they sound different. They can have their friends guess what is inside the shaker and then open it to see if they are right. The gardening table remains.

Sensorimotor Level

1. Encourage children at the sensorimotor level to explore and dig in the dirt table or in a separate tub of dirt on the floor.

2. Children at this level may not have enough strength or understanding to shell the Indian corn; however, they can feel the corn, drop the ears in a container, and explore and wave the husks around so that they make noise.
3. These children may love crawling into the box. You should be very cautious, however, with children at this level who mouth objects. Pour out all small objects before the child crawls into the box.
4. Many of these children may not like having paint applied to their faces. Let them fingerpaint in orange paint instead.
5. The feely box will be fun for these children and allow opportunities for labeling the items pulled out. Keep the items basic.

Functional Level

1. The children at the functional level can work on a sequence: a) dig a hole, b) take out a seed, c) plant it, and d) cover it up.
2. Label each step with short phrases or sentences (e.g., "Let's dig a hole," "Now you are planting") for these children.
3. Have these children work on counting to three or four in both the planting and the shelling activities.
4. These children may enjoy crawling into and out of the box. Encourage a sequence: a) crawl in, b) put something in the basket, and c) then crawl out.
5. Facilitate the sequence of making the noisemakers, and label the parts (e.g., "seeds," "top") and sounds (e.g., "loud," "soft").
6. Children at this level may enjoy putting paint on their faces, but do not expect it to represent something.
7. Try having these children predict what they feel in the box to encourage the development of mental representations and language.

Symbolic Level

1. Encourage children at the symbolic level to classify the different types of seeds and plant in rows or clusters of like kinds. They can then label the rows with the signs they made.
2. Encourage these children to count the seeds and beans as they plant them or dig them up. They can also try counting all of the kernels in the corn container.
3. The box can represent an extension of the forest for these children and can be incorporated into the story sequence. Discuss what they are finding as well as how to classify herbs, nuts, and seeds.
4. Encourage children at this level who make sound shakers to compare the sounds (e.g., "louder," "harder," "noisier"). They can also try to identify which is which from the sounds.

5. With the face painting and hand shadow puppets, encourage the representation of actual things with these children.
6. For children at this level who are beginning to recognize words, write several words on a piece of paper and have them identify the item in the feely box by pointing to the correct word.

MOTOR AREA

This area is combined with music and movement for the first week. You may want to do this as a whole class at the end of center time rather than as a separate center. (As described in the *Teacher's Guide,* the centers discussed in each module may comprise only part of a day. Additional reading, music, or other activities may follow.) During the second week, motor activities are focused on a platform swing that has been transformed into a spiderweb. This is intended to be an area to which children may choose to go during center time. Additional activities for the center are also included for variation.

WEEK 1

Day 1 Sing "If You're Afraid and You Know It" to the tune of "If You're Happy and You Know It," and substitute the words in the story. You may want to have the children take the gloves and hat brought from home out of their cubbies to wear during the song.

Day 2 Play slow music. Give the children scarves to wave in the air. Then everyone can move like trees in the wind, first a slow wind and then a fast wind. Use the scarves as props as you walk, hop, skip, and run. Those who have difficulty moving their lower limbs may use the scarves as the action instrument.

Day 3 Use different instruments (e.g., bongos, drums, sticks, tambourines) to accompany loud, pounding music (e.g., *Beethoven's Fifth Symphony*) to pretend you are mad (stomp around), worried (tiptoe), frightened (shaking and running), and so forth.

Day 4 Have the children use musical instruments (e.g., tambourines, drums, horns, whistles). Move around in a circle as you make scary noises (e.g., the wind shaking the trees, a dog howling, a door banging).

Day 5 Play Old Lady Says. Using the instruments and scarves, let the children choose the movements and sounds they want to make in the same style as Simon Says (e.g., "Old lady says, 'Be a tree'"; "Old Lady says, 'Move slowly'").

WEEK 2

Day 1 If available from an occupational therapist or physical therapist, borrow a platform swing to include in the classroom. This piece of equipment is especially helpful for children who benefit from vestibular stimulation, but most children love it! Wrap string around the swing to represent a spiderweb so that the children will need to maneuver around the string to get on the platform. Using some of the music from the previous week, they can pretend they are trees swaying in the wind. If a swing is not available, the spiderweb can be made on some sort of climber, and the children can pretend they are climbing a tree to look for scary things.

Day 2 Repeat the spiderweb on the swing or the climber. Find a large, inflatable pumpkin to roll at the scarecrow. Score points for hitting the scarecrow's feet. The inflatable pumpkin (available at drug stores around Halloween) can also be used for playing catch. Facilitate the interaction between children who are typically more isolated. Children of all levels should be able to push or throw the inflatable pumpkin.

Day 3 Repeat the previous day's activities. Let the children initiate the games and make up the rules. If you are using a platform swing, you may want to set a timer for 2 minutes and limit the number of children on the swing to three. Let one of the children on the swing be responsible for counting the number of children on the platform and listening for the timer to indicate when it is time to get off and let on other children.

Day 4 Have the materials out from the previous days from which the children may choose. Put orange chalk near the chalkboard, and demonstrate how to draw a *giant* pumpkin, moving your whole arm in *big* circles. Then let the children go to it. Even coloring in the pumpkins, if they decide to do so, will require arm movements from the shoulder.

Day 5 Repeat the previous day's activities.

Sensorimotor Level

1. Help the children at the sensorimotor level to imitate the actions with the others as the class sings "If You're Afraid and You Know It."
2. Children at this level will be able to move with the music and be able to say or sign the word MUSIC.
3. The pumpkin roll and catch is appropriate for these children, but keeping track of points is not.
4. These children will probably not be able to draw with large arm movements on the board, but they may enjoy marking or scribbling on the board, which is great.
5. Swinging on the platform swing will provide vestibular input and work on balance and equilibrium. Encourage these children to use words or

signs for GO and STOP. Give these children wait time, and watch for and acknowledge any communicative act or sound.

Functional Level

1. Children at the functional level will be able to incorporate the descriptive words, such as "fast" and "slow." Work on increasing these children's vocabulary comprehension.
2. Incorporate counting into the pumpkin roll activity for these children.
3. Drawing large objects on the board is a very good activity for these children as it uses one of the body's key points of control, the shoulder. Controlled movements here will aid the development of fine motor skills as well.
4. These children will probably enjoy the vestibular input provided by the platform swing. Encourage them to count the three peers on the swing and to communicate in words or phrases, such as, "I'm ready," and, "Let's go."

Symbolic Level

1. Children at the symbolic level will be able to model the actions for others.
2. The pumpkin roll activity can incorporate not only counting but also keeping score and making something into a game with rules (e.g., "How many turns does each child get?" "How high shall we go?").
3. If these children choose to draw giant pumpkins, encourage them to label the pumpkin with their name or dictate a sentence to you to write under the pumpkin on the chalkboard.
4. These children can help monitor the number of children on the platform swing, learn how to set the timer, and help control the movement of the swing. Work on comparative terms (e.g., "fast, faster, fastest"; "slow, slower, slowest").

FLOOR PLAY

Floor play in this module includes blocks, puzzles, and miniature characters.

WEEK 1

Day 1 The children can use large blocks to build the old lady's house or a fence around her garden. Puzzles of people or clothing can be laid out on the floor as well as switch toys (e.g., pumpkins with flashing lights), scarecrow dolls with clothes for dressing them (a Raggedy Andy will work), and pumpkin buckets to use as containers into which small items (e.g., clothespins, small blocks) can be dropped.

Day 2 Legos and other types of small blocks can be put out for the children to build a miniature scenario of the story. Add small characters, such as an old lady doll (any female miniature or a small Halloween witch), doll clothing, a small plastic pumpkin, and a miniature scarecrow (found in Halloween and seasonal material sections in hobby shops). You may need to assist in the first stages of play with these materials. Demonstrate how the materials relate to the pictures in the book. Let one of the children manipulate the old lady doll while you or the other children play the parts of the clothing. Continue with the puzzles, miniature dolls, pumpkins, and switch toys.

Day 3 Repeat the miniature scenario with the same materials from the previous day. You should need to facilitate the miniature scenario less than the previous day.

Day 4 Repeat the miniature scenario. Play the Shoe Hunt game. Have different pairs of shoes and boots out in the middle of the floor. Hide one of each pair around the room, and let the children find them. Once they find a shoe or a boot, they can take it to the center of the room and find its match. Line up each pair, and let the children count the individual shoes and the pairs. Talk about "pairs" and things that come in pairs (e.g., eyes, ears, shoes).

Day 5 Repeat the miniature scenario. Repeat the Shoe Hunt game.

WEEK 2

The same materials from Week 1 are placed out for Week 2. Facilitation is needed for children who have not yet chosen this area. Facilitation is also needed for the children at the sensorimotor and functional levels to "bump them up" to higher levels of actions and language. In addition, some of the following games can be added.

Day 1 Play the Match the Clothing game. Place a pile of clothing in the middle of the floor, consisting of three pairs of shoes, three shirts, three pairs of pants, three sets of gloves, and three hats. Each of the three sets of clothing can be three sizes (i.e., doll size, toddler size, and preschool size). Let the children sort the clothing and line them up into sets. Repeat the puzzles, miniature dolls, pumpkins, and switch toys.

Day 2 The Match the Clothing game can also be made into a board game. Before class, make a game board out of a square piece of cardboard. Place a dot in the center of the board, and draw lines equal distance apart radiating from the center. (The number of sections can vary depending on the level of the children in the class.) In each section, draw a line drawing of one of the following: a shoe, a pair of pants, a shirt, a hat, and a glove. Make each drawing big or small, and label the item. Let several children lie on their stomachs on the floor around the game board to color in the pictures on the board. Tell them they are helping to make the Big and Small game. When the children are done coloring the game board, attach an arrow to the center with a paper fastener through the arrow, a washer, the board, and another washer. Then spread the legs of the fastener on the back of the board. You are now ready to play the Big and Little game with a small group of children. Place a pile of big and small clothing near the board or in a box next to the board. (Place it farther away if you want the children to have to get up and move to get to the clothes.) Give each child a small, plastic pumpkin or another container, such as an empty margarine dish. Let each child, in turn, spin the arrow so that it points to a piece of clothing. Have them name what they found if they are able, such as "a big shirt," and go to the box and find the item. Let the rest of the group decide whether the child is correct. Replace the item in the pile or box. If the item is correct, give the child a small token or flower to put in his or her pumpkin. Continue until the children tire of the game. Repeat the puzzles, miniature dolls, pumpkins, and switch toys.

Day 3 Have the children help nail together three sets of wood strips to form three crosses that match in size to the clothing. Then repeat the Match the Clothing game with modification. This time let the children stuff the clothing with newspapers, dress the crossed sticks with the set of clothing that matches its size, and pin the clothing together. These scarecrows can be "planted" in coffee cans filled with dirt or rocks. Repeat the puzzles, miniature dolls, pumpkins, and switch toys.

Day 4 Finish the scarecrows by letting the children make heads for them. Bring in an empty pint, quart, and half-gallon milk container. Let the children cover each container with orange construction paper. Attach the paper to the containers with glue or tape. Then let three of the children draw faces on the cartons. Set these on top of the scarecrows made the previous day, and top with the appropriate size hat. Repeat the puzzles, miniature dolls, pumpkins, and switch toys.

Day 5 Play a board game, such as "Don't Spill the Beans" or "Farm Families" (both from Milton Bradley).

Sensorimotor Level

1. The children at the sensorimotor level will enjoy using a variety of materials to drop in the pumpkin bucket, such as things that are loud (e.g., blocks), things that make a different sound (e.g., squeak toys), and things that feel unique to the touch (e.g., Koosh balls).
2. Label both the object (e.g., "block") and the sound (e.g., "bang") for these children.
3. Switch toys, such as a battery-operated Halloween pumpkin that makes noise or a battery-operated animal, can be used so that children at this level can be incorporated into the dramatic play. They can activate the devices in the forest as the old lady walks through.

Functional Level

1. Use puzzles with separate holes for pieces with children at the functional level. Encourage them to complete the puzzles.
2. Encourage the use of miniatures, even though the children at this level may not completely relate them to the story. Prompt the sequence of actions and sounds.
3. These children will also enjoy the switch toys.

Symbolic Level

1. The dramatization of the story with the miniature scenario will allow the children at the symbolic level to practice representational thinking involving all of the characters under their direction.
2. Encourage these children to use the script with the action sequence.
3. Encourage these children to make up new parts to the story and improvise.

4. More difficult, multipiece puzzles are appropriate for these children depending on each child's ability level.
5. Encourage these children to use switch toys in cooperation with children at the other levels. They can model and take turns.

TABLE PLAY

WEEK 1

Day 1 Using Popsicle sticks and paper faces and hats, make a puppet scarecrow. The Popsicle stick is the body and the handle of the puppet. A small branch or twig can be glued across the Popsicle stick for arms. The children can cut out circles and use markers to make the face. They can then design and cut out a hat. (Do not be surprised if they turn out rather oddly shaped!)

Day 2 Repeat the previous day's activity. If desired, the children can also make a little old lady puppet. Have some scraps of material or wallpaper for making a dress to glue onto the Popsicle stick. Encourage the children to interact with each other with their puppets by having the little old lady tell the scarecrow, "I'm not afraid of you."

Make a paper bag head for the life-size scarecrow. Stuff the paper bag with newspaper, and have the children make a face on it. Top it with an old hat, and it is ready to go on the scarecrow.

Day 3 Make sock puppet scarecrows. Have the children stuff the toe of the sock with newspaper. Then wrap a rubber band around the sock to make the scarecrow's neck (you will need to help with this part). If desired, a paper or fabric hat can be cut out and glued on. Cut a hole on each side of the sock under the head. The children can now add a face, put their hands in, and have a scarecrow puppet.

Day 4 Repeat making the sock or Popsicle puppets. Cut opposite sides out of a box for a theater. The children can make up a play or reenact the story with their puppets and some doll clothes for additional props.

Day 5 Use the line drawings of the old lady and other items in the story that can be found in the appendix of the *Teacher's Guide.* Photocopy and cut out the pieces. Some children may be able to cut them out by themselves, others may need help. (You can use flannel, but it is difficult to cut). Let the children color the pieces and then glue a piece of flannel or Velcro (Velcro actually works better) to the back. These pieces can now be used to tell a story on a flannel board. (See the Literacy Center, Week 2, Day 1.)

Use a picture chart so that the children can follow the directions to make orange juice Popsicles. The chart should show an ice cube tray and a pitcher of orange juice as well as the action of pouring the juice into the tray and putting the tray in the freezer. These will be used for snack on Day 1 of Week 2.

Day 1 Make orange playdough.

ORANGE PLAYDOUGH

2 cups of flour
1 cup of salt
2 tablespoons of salad oil
Water
Orange Kool-Aid (instead of food coloring)

Mix all of the ingredients together in a large bowl. The children can take turns adding the ingredients and stirring. Then they can knead the playdough with their hands and smell it. The Kool-Aid will give the playdough an orange smell. Let the children each have a chunk to pat, roll, shape, and cut up. Although the children should decide what they want to make, you could suggest rolling the dough into pumpkins, cutting it into shapes, and so forth.

Day 2 Bring out the playdough made the previous day. Let the children experiment with different Halloween cookie cutters. Talk about which ones are scary things and what the little old lady would say.

Day 3 Repeat playing with the playdough. This time you can model making clothing with the playdough (e.g., "I'm going to make a pair of pants like the ones that followed the little old lady. Let's see, a pair of pants has two legs. What are you going to make?"). Whatever the children choose to make is fine.

Day 4 Draw jack-o'-lantern or old lady faces on paper plates (orange plates would be great!). Make them into puzzles. For those who are not attached to keeping their plates in one piece, cut the plate into two pieces, with some cut into two wavy pieces, some cut jagged, and so forth just so that they are all different. Write or have the children write the children's names on the back of each piece. Then mix them up, deal out two pieces to each child, and let them trade until they find their own pieces to make the puzzle fit together.

Day 5 Repeat making puzzles for those who did not make them the previous day. Bring out the puzzles the children made who return to the area. They can make another puzzle or just play the game with their puzzles from the previous day. Using the Jell-O Jigglers made in the Science and Math Center the previous day, let the children use cookie cutters to cut out Halloween figures. If possible, make two pans of them so that the children at the sensorimotor level can experiment with their hands and spoons.

Sensorimotor Level

1. Making representational puppet figures is inappropriate for the children at the sensorimotor level. Redirect them to another center, or bring over the plastic pumpkin and let them drop in Popsicle sticks and dump them.

2. These children can help stuff the paper bag with paper for the scarecrow head.
3. Children at this level who are not mouthing objects can squeeze and manipulate the playdough.

Functional Level

1. Children at the functional level can, with support, engage in most of the activities. You can help move these children into representational thinking through the drawing of faces and puppet play.
2. Support these children in playing out the sequence of actions in each event.
3. Label objects and actions (e.g., "scarecrow," "lady," "cut," "paste") for these children.
4. Encourage these children to make a representation of an object with the playdough.

Symbolic Level

1. All of the activities in this area will encourage representation and sequencing by the children at the symbolic level.
2. Encourage these children to problem-solve as they work on the scarecrow puppets (e.g., "What should we do for a . . . ?").
3. The flannel board is a multistep activity that promotes sequential thinking and emerging literacy skills in children. Emphasize, for these children, the storytelling as the characters are made. Incorporate language related to *why* the little old lady was afraid, how it becomes clear that she was getting more frightened, and how she overcame her fear.
4. Prompt these children to use the picture chart while making the playdough.

OUTDOOR PLAY

WEEK 1

Day 1 Play the Walk, Stop, and Run game. Let the children line up facing the playground fence or the building. Explain that the game is like the old lady in the book who walks through the woods, stops to meet the clothing, then runs when the pumpkin head says, "BOO!" Tell the children to walk slowly toward the fence, to stop walking when you shout, "STOP!" and to run when you shout, "BOO!" Children who cannot walk or run can be pushed in a wheelchair or pulled in a wagon by a peer. Vary the commands so that the children have to listen carefully. When all of the children reach the fence or wall, have them walk or run back to you. Free play.

Day 2 Repeat the Walk, Stop, and Run game. This time let the children take turns being the person who shouts out commands. This will undoubtedly be more chaotic but just as much fun! Free play.

Day 3 Hide small, plastic pumpkins around the playground, and let the children search for them. Free play.

Day 4 Hang a clothesline outside between two trees or between the supports on a swing set. Bring out a basket of clothing and a bag of clothespins. Let the children hang the clothing on the line using clothespins. The children can pretend that they are hanging clean clothes out to dry. They will enjoy hanging them up and taking them down over and over. Free play.

Day 5 Repeat the hanging of clothing on a clothesline. Free play.

WEEK 2

Day 1 Take gardening tools outside to the sandbox area. Let the children plant seeds (or small rocks) in the "garden." Free play.

Day 2 Repeat gardening in the sandbox. Take some of the clothing outside and dress a broom stick as a scarecrow to put near the sandbox. Free play.

Day 3 Play Old Lady Says, like Simon Says. Use the actions in the story, such as "Old Lady says, 'Clomp your feet'" or "Old Lady says, 'Shake your hands.'" Let the children take turns being the Old Lady. Free play.

Day 4 Take a box of clothing outside, and let the children dress up and pretend to be scarecrows. They may want to dress you up, too! You also could make this a structured game. Let the children identify "What's missing on the scarecrow" and help you put on each piece of clothing that the children name. You need to be a ham and act very floppy so that the children will have to work hard to get the scarecrow dressed. Play Scarecrow Says (e.g., "Scarecrow says, 'Take off your hat'"). Free play.

Day 5 Play the Broom Ball game. Have the children stand in a circle. Let one child stand in the middle with a broom. Let another child roll a ball toward the child in the center. The child in the center is to use the broom to avoid getting hit by the ball, sweeping the ball aside to another child. Have the children count aloud each time the child in the center strikes the ball and returns it to a child in the circle. The child who gets the ball as the number 10 is called gets to become the person in the center with the broom. Free play.

Sensorimotor Level

1. The children at the sensorimotor level will not understand the rules of the Walk, Stop, and Run game or the Old Lady Says game, but they will imitate their friends. Do not worry if they do not exactly follow their friends. You may be able to accompany these children to help them understand the words by demonstrating and helping them to act out the actions.
2. Pair these children with a peer from one of the other levels on the search for the pumpkin.
3. Hanging up the clothes or dressing the scarecrow may be too difficult for these children, but they may be able to hand the clothing to their peers or release the clothing from the clothesline.
4. Give these children tools to use in the sandbox.
5. Let these children roll the ball toward the child in the center while playing the Broom Ball game.

Functional Level

1. Encourage the children at the functional level to watch their peers and listen for the words "Walk," "Stop," or "Run" during the Walk, Stop, and Run game. If children are present who cannot walk or run, then the words can be changed to "Stop" and "Go" so that the children will feel free to move in whatever way they can.
2. Give these children clues to help them find the pumpkins (e.g., "Look behind the trees").
3. Show these children how to use clothespins (use different types of clothespins depending on children's fine motor skills.) Let them hang up washcloths if real clothing is too difficult to manipulate.

4. Encourage these children in the sandbox to pretend to plant seeds (rocks) and find them again.
5. Let these children help dress you as a scarecrow. You can encourage these children to tell those dressing the scarecrow what to do with the clothing.
6. When playing the Broom Ball game, give the children small-size brooms to increase their ability to be successful in hitting the ball.

Symbolic Level

1. Let the children at the symbolic level take turns giving directions in the Walk, Stop, and Run game and the Old Lady Says game. Relate the games to the actions of the old lady in the story.
2. Have these children pretend to be the old lady hanging out the clothing to dry, as in the picture in the beginning of the story. Discuss how the air and the wind dry the clothes. Wet clothing may pose more of a challenge to untangle and hang!
3. Show these children how to use a stick to draw a line in the sand to form a "planting row." Then they can use the garden tools to plant seeds or rocks.
4. These children will enjoy dressing you as a scarecrow! You may tease these children by putting the clothing on the wrong body parts and letting them correct the errors.
5. Have these children count the number of Broom Ball strokes until 10 is reached and the child in the center can switch places with one of the children on the outside of the circle.

SNACK

The snacks in this module include many new tastes for the children. Some incorporate spices or herbs. Encourage the children to try the new flavors. If their peers are trying new things, then they may, too. (Have simple backups available in case you meet resistance.)

WEEK 1

Day 1

Oral motor: Some older people lose their teeth. Let the children look in small mirrors at their teeth. Have the children smile, open wide and look inside, and move their lips so that the children can see their gums. Then have the children pull their lips over their teeth and pretend they have no teeth. Repeat several times. Talk about why it is important to brush your teeth so that you do not get cavities or lose your teeth.

Snack: Pretend that the little old lady goes into the woods to pick herbs, spices, nuts, and seeds. Give the children crackers, and let them spread cream cheese on the cracker. Sprinkle different spices on top of the crackers for the children to taste (e.g., chives, nutmeg, parsley). Have apple juice to drink.

Day 2

Oral motor: Repeat having the children examine their mouths and teeth in the mirror and making toothless faces.

Snack: Serve pumpkin seeds, either purchased or baked. (Save the seeds from the pumpkin carved in the Science and Math Center previously.) Roast and salt them for snack. Serve with water to drink.

Day 3

Oral motor: Sing "Ten Little Pumpkins" to the tune of "Ten Little Indians." Emphasize the movement of the lips and tongues on each syllable. Add finger movements.

Snack: Serve creamed corn, and talk about how the little old lady grew corn in her garden. Serve milk to drink.

Day 4

Oral motor: Have the children use their lips and tongue to make sound effects for the actions in the story. For example, for "CLOMP, CLOMP," have the children make a clicking sound with their tongue; for "WIGGLE, WIGGLE," move the tongue up and down; for "SHAKE, SHAKE," move the tongue side to side; for "CLAP, CLAP," smack the lips together and apart; for "NOD, NOD," have the tongue go in and out of the mouth and when the tongue is out, try to touch the chin with the tongue; and for "BOO, BOO," make the lips into an "O" and exaggerate the "ooo" sound.

Snack: Sprinkle herbs on cream cheese spread on crackers with lemonade to drink.

Day 5 Oral motor: Repeat the lip and tongue movements that go with the actions of the story.

Snack: Serve cinnamon rice cakes and apple juice. Discuss how spices make things better.

WEEK 2

Day 1 Oral motor: Make sounds like the wind blowing in the woods (e.g., "whoo," "whish"): make a soft, gentle wind; a hard, fast wind; a loud wind, and so forth. Let the children generate how each of the winds should sound.

Snack: Serve orange juice Popsicles made in Table Play the previous week. Serve with water to drink.

Day 2 Oral motor: Show the children how to make a pretend milkshake with your mouth. You can demonstrate puffing out your cheeks and lips with air and swishing the air around in your mouth (like rinsing the mouth with mouthwash). Talk about how you are going to make a milkshake, and shake the milk around. If the classroom has a sink, the children can try rinsing out their mouths with water or mouthwash! Mouthwash will provide increased sensory input.

Snack: Make a milkshake. Place the ingredients (ice cream and milk) in several small containers with tight lids, and have the children take turns shaking the container. Shake it in different directions, up and down and sideways. Talk about what shaking means and how the shirt in the story shakes. Talk about what other things shake (e.g., leaves, dogs' tails). Use straws to drink the shake to encourage lip closure and sucking. Water may be desired after drinking the shakes. Again, provide straws.

Day 3 Oral motor: Repeat the previous day's "mouthwash" movements.

Snack: Serve the pumpkin bread made in the Science and Math Center with milk to drink. Talk about how the pumpkin changes as it becomes bread.

Day 4 Make jack-o'-lantern faces that are happy, sad, mean, mad, scared, and so forth.

Snack: Serve corn muffins made in the Science and Math Center and orange juice to drink. Discuss what happened to the corn.

Day 5 Make jack-o'-lantern faces that are happy, sad, mean, mad, scared, and so forth.

Snack: Serve the granola muffins made in the Math and Science Center. Have milk to drink. Compare the tastes and textures of the muffins to the corn muffins.

Sensorimotor Level

1. Let the children at the sensorimotor level imitate the mouth movements to the best of their abilities. You may be able to assist the children if they tolerate facial touching.
2. If a child at this level is unable to imitate the movements, a washcloth can be provided for the child (or for you) to rub and pat the mouth.
3. Encourage these children to use straws to drink to encourage lip closure and sucking.
4. Encourage these children to use a prehensile grasp when eating finger foods.
5. Label all foods and actions for these children.
6. Let these children assist their peers in serving.

Functional Level

1. As with children at the sensorimotor level, children at the functional level should be encouraged to imitate mouth movements.
2. Have these children use a mirror and their hands to help make the faces. Watching the peers in the class will also provide a model.
3. Encourage these children to talk about what they are doing and eating.
4. When serving, these children can count the children, cups, plates, and so forth.

Symbolic Level

1. Let the children at the symbolic level lead the actions and mouth movements. They can experiment with what the various faces might look like before you provide an example. (In some cases, theirs may be *better!*)
2. Children at this level can try to recall the steps they took to make the recipes in the Science and Math Center. They may want to refer to the picture charts to assist them. This will provide additional practice in reading the charts.
3. Have these children try to guess which flavors they are tasting. They can point out the seeds and spices they can see.
4. Have these children take advantage of opportunities to count when serving (e.g., "How many children are usually there?" "Who is missing?" "How many cupcakes do we need?"). They can also help cut the servings of bread into "equal" pieces.

HOW TO INVOLVE FAMILIES

Families can be involved in the story of *The Little Old Lady Who Was Not Afraid of Anything* in many ways. A week or so before the book is read, send caregivers a letter letting them know what you will be reading. Include with the letter a list of materials that they may be able to help supply, the vocabulary list from the beginning of the module, and the planning sheets from the beginning of the module. The following is a sample of the first letter:

Date

Dear families,

Next week we will begin the book *The Little Old Lady Who Was Not Afraid of Anything,* by Linda Williams. This story fits with the Halloween holiday, as it involves a jack-o'-lantern, but it does not address Halloween specifically. We, therefore, hope this book will be acceptable to any families who do not participate in Halloween. The story is about an old lady who sets out to gather herbs, spices, seeds, and nuts from the forest. It is dark when she starts home. She soon discovers that she is being followed by a pair of shoes that go, "CLOMP, CLOMP!" She is not afraid but hurries on. Subsequently she is followed by a pair of pants, a shirt, two gloves, a hat, and a pumpkin head, all of which make scary noises. They chase her home and try to scare her, but she is not to be frightened. Instead, she recommends they stay in her garden and scare the crows away.

This is a story about confronting your fears, and we will use it to let the children talk about things that frighten them and how they can be brave, too. We will use various aspects of the story to help us study body parts and clothing; seeds, herbs, and spices; and body movements. We will be dramatizing the sequence in the story and helping the children begin to predict what comes next. We will make up our own stories and create books of our own. In the Science and Math Center, we will be studying seeds and comparing and measuring different sizes of clothing. We will also be making several of our snacks that involve elements from the story, such as corn, pumpkin, and spices. (Please be sure to let us know if your child has any allergies.) Cooking will allow the children to follow a picture chart recipe and to measure and combine different ingredients to see how they change in the cooking process. In addition, we will be doing a variety of movement activities, involving moving slowly and fast, moving like the wind, and so forth. We will be adapting games such as Simon Says to Old Lady Says and incorporating the movements in the story.

What can you do to communicate with your child about what we are doing at school?

1. If possible, obtain a copy of the book so that you can read it to your child; and, as the week progresses, let your child begin to read it to you, predicting what will happen next and incorporating the actions of the story.
2. You can do the same type of size sequencing we are doing at school by including your child in sorting the clothes for the laundry and identifying the colors, the piece of clothing, and who wears it.

3. Let your child help you remove the clothes from the dryer and sort them into big and little piles of Daddy's clothes, Mommy's clothes, brother's/sister's clothes, and so forth. Your child may be able to begin to sort the clothing into categories, such as all of the shirts or all of the socks.
4. Folding may be more difficult, but let them try to fold the washcloths and socks to increase their ability to plan.
5. Involve your child in grocery shopping for the items you need. Classify the items as fruits, vegetables, meats, spices, and so forth.
6. Let your child help you measure the ingredients when cooking. Talk about what the ingredients are and which ones are spices, seeds, nuts, and so forth.
7. When all of those catalogs come in the mail, look at them with your child and identify different types of clothing, when it is worn, whether it is big or little, whom it would fit, what the colors are, and so forth.
8. When your child brings home a book or project from school, have him or her tell you how he or she made it. Ask your child what he or she did "first," "next," and "last." Point out what your favorite thing about the project is so that you are talking about specific aspects rather than just saying it is "good" or "nice." This will encourage your child to talk to you about what was done and to say how he or she feels about the work.

Attached is a list of some of the vocabulary and concepts we will be using. You may want to try to use some of them at home, too. We are also sending the planning sheets for the 2 weeks so that you will know what your child is doing and can talk about the day's activities. Keep in mind that not all children will be doing the same activities, as the children choose what they want to do, and some activities are more appropriate for different children. We have also included a list of items that we will be needing for all of these activities. If you can provide any of them, we would appreciate your contribution to the classroom:

- Clothing catalogs
- Different sizes of empty milk cartons
- Empty (clean) Styrofoam meat trays
- Empty Pringles cans
- Fabric samples and wallpaper samples
- Halloween spiderwebbing
- Large box for the children to climb in
- Old clothing of different sizes, particularly pants, shirts, shoes, gloves, and hats (put your name inside and we will return them)
- Old socks for puppets
- Packages of seeds
- Paper plates
- Plastic wrap
- Seed catalogs
- Small, brown paper bags
- Sponges
- Wood strips to make small scarecrows

Thank you!

Sincerely,

Prior to the second week, send another letter home to the family to report on the last week's activities and introduce the coming week. The following is a sample letter:

Date

Dear families,

We are continuing our module on *The Little Old Lady Who Was Not Afraid of Anything.* The children have been having fun acting out the story. You may be hearing the refrains from the story. When your child is getting dressed, you may want to incorporate these actions. We've also been pretending to plant seeds. If you have some seeds at home, plant some in an old egg carton your child fills with dirt. (If you plant herbs, you can use them in your cooking later!) Let him or her water the seeds every day and watch them grow.

We are also carving a pumpkin and using pumpkin-shaped cookie cutters with playdough. Here is a recipe for playdough that you can make at home. The orange Kool-Aid gives it a fragrant smell.

ORANGE PLAYDOUGH

2 cups of flour
1 cup of salt
2 tablespoons of salad oil
Water
Orange Kool-Aid (instead of food coloring)

Mix all of the ingredients together and knead. Let your child help with all of the steps. Add water a little at a time until the dough is the right consistency. Use a rolling pin or jar to flatten the clay; use other kitchen utensils and cookie cutters to experiment with the clay.

Have fun!

Sincerely,

MORE SUGGESTIONS

Books

(*Note:* Titles listed below that are preceded by an asterisk are similar to the storybook featured in this module and may be your most appropriate substitutes with modifications if you are unable to locate the recommended storybook.)

Alborough, J. (1992). *Where's my teddy?* Cambridge, MA: Candlewick Press.

Alborough, J. (1994). *It's the bear!* Cambridge, MA: Candlewick Press.

Bang, M. (1980). *The grey lady and the strawberry snatcher.* New York: Four Winds Press.

Brown, R. (1991). *A dark, dark tale.* Albany, NY: Delmar Publishers.

Crowe, R.L. (1976). *Clyde monster.* New York: E.P. Dutton.

Fox, M. (1989). *Night noises.* San Diego: Harcourt Brace Jovanovich.

Galdone, P. (1984). *The teeny-tiny woman: A ghost story.* New York: Clarion Books.

Henkes, K. (1987). *Sheila Rae, the brave.* New York: Greenwillow Books.

Mayer, M. (1983). *All by myself.* New York: Golden Press.

Mayer, M. (1983). *I was so mad.* New York: Golden Press.

Mayer, M. (1968). *There's a nightmare in my closet.* New York: Dial Books for Young Readers.

Mosel, A. (1972). *The funny little woman.* New York: Dutton.

*Polacco, P. (1990). *Thunder cake.* New York: Philomel Books.

Sendak, M. (1992). *Where the wild things are.* New York: HarperFestival.

Seuss, Dr. (1996). *My many colored days.* New York: Alfred A. Knopf.

*Westcott, N.B. (1980). *I know an old lady who swallowed a fly.* Boston: Little, Brown.

Fingerplays, Songs, and Games

FIVE LITTLE MONSTERS JUMPING ON THE BED (variation of "Five Little Monkeys")

Five little monsters jumping on the bed.
[Move fingers up and down on palm of hand.]

One fell off and bumped his head.
[Rub head.]

Mama called the doctor, and the doctor said,
[Pretend to use the phone.]

"That's what you get for jumping on the bed!"
[Shake finger.]

Four little monsters . . . (and so on)

Three little monsters . . . (and so on)

Two little monsters . . . (and so on)

One little monster jumping on the bed.
He fell off and bumped his head.
Mama called the doctor,
And the doctor said,
"No more monsters jumping on the bed!"

(Adapted from Cole, J., & Calmenson, S. [1991]. *The eentsy, weentsy spider: Fingerplays and action rhymes* [pp. 38–39]. New York: Mulberry Books.)

MONSTER IN THE MIDDLE GAME

One child stands in the center of the circle. The other children pass a small object and chant "Monster, monster, where's your broom? Somebody stole it from your room." The child in the middle then attempts to guess who is holding the object.

MAKING RAIN

Clouds roll in,
[Rub hands together.]

Drip, drops, splatter,
[Snap fingers.]

They're getting bigger and faster.
[Slap knees slowly.]

Thunder! A cloudburst!
[Slap knees hard and fast.]

[Slow it down and repeat the cycle.]

THE LOUD AND QUIET GAME

Children think of and name things that make loud and quiet sounds. They then act out and/or create the sounds.

THIS OLD LADY (same as "This Old Man")

This old lady,
[Hands on hips.]

She played one.
[Hold up one finger.]

She played knick-knack on her thumb,
[With pointer finger, tap thumb of opposite hand.]

With a nick
[Slap right thigh with right hand.]

Nack
[Slap left thigh with left hand.]

Paddy
[Slap left shoulder with right hand.]

Whack
[Slap right shoulder with left hand.]

Give the dog a bone,
[Hands out in front, palms up.]

This old lady came rolling home.
[Roll hands over each other; then thumbs point back over shoulders.]

2. This old lady, she played two,
[Hold up two fingers.]

She played knick-knack on my shoe
[Point to shoe.]

[And so on]

3. Three . . . on my knee [Tap knee.]
4. Four . . . on my door [Tap forehead.]
5. Five . . . on my hive [Tap fist.]
6. Six . . . on my sticks [Tap pointer fingers together.]
7. Seven . . . up in heaven [Point up to heaven.]
8. Eight . . . on my gate [Tap forearm in front of you.]
9. Nine . . . on my spine [Tap on backbone.]
10. Ten . . . once again [Clap hands.]

(Adapted from Cole, J., & Calmenson, S. [1991]. *The eentsy, weentsy spider: Fingerplays and action rhymes* [pp. 46–47]. New York: Mulberry Books.)

TWO LITTLE BLACKBIRDS

Two little blackbirds sitting on a hill;
[Two hands closed, thumbs up to resemble birds.]

One named Jack; one named Jill.
[Slightly raise one hand and then the other.]

Fly away, Jack; fly away, Jill.
[Right hand is opened, raised above head, same with left.]

Come back, Jack; come back, Jill.
[Right hand and left back to original position.]

(Reprinted from "Ring a Ring o' Roses" [p. 124], published by the Flint Public Library, 1026 E. Kearsley Street, Flint, MI 48502 [810] 232-7111.)

JACK-O-LANTERN

I am a pumpkin, big and round.
[Use arms to show size of pumpkin.]

Once upon a time I grew on the ground.
[Point to the ground.]

Now I have a mouth, two eyes, and a nose.
[Point to each feature on own face.]

What are they for, do you suppose?
[Right forefinger to forehead—thinking gesture.]

When I have a candle inside shining bright
[Hold up right forefinger.]

I'll be a jack-o-lantern on Halloween night.
[Thumb in armpits—bragging gesture.]

(Reprinted from "Ring a Ring o' Roses" [p. 66], published by the Flint Public Library, 1026 E. Kearsley Street, Flint, MI 48502 [810] 232-7111.)

THE EENTSY WEENTSY SPIDER

The eentsy, weentsy spider climbed up the water spout.
[Put first fingers to thumbs and raise arms as you alternate switching the thumbs and fingers one at a time.]

Down came the rain
[Move fingers as you lower arms and hands.]

And washed the spider out.
[Spread hands and arms outward from the center.]

Out came the sun
[Make a circle with your arms around face.]

And dried up all the rain.
[Spread hands and arms outward from the center.]

And the eentsy, weentsy spider climbed up the spout again.

(Reprinted from Cole, J., & Calmenson, S. [1991]. *The eentsy, weentsy spider: Fingerplays and action rhymes* [p. 25]. New York: Mulberry Books.)

IF YOU'RE HAPPY [OR AFRAID] AND YOU KNOW IT

If you're happy and you know it, clap your hands.
[Clap hands.]

If you're happy and you know it, clap your hands.
[Clap hands.]

If you're happy and you know it,
Then your face is 'gonna' show it,

If you're happy and you know it, clap your hands.
[Clap hands.]

Repeat with other words and actions.

(Partially reprinted from "Ring a Ring o' Roses" [p. 62], published by the Flint Public Library, 1026 E. Kearsley Street, Flint, MI 48502 [810] 232-7111.)

TEN LITTLE PUMPKINS

One little, two little, three little pumpkins,
Four little, five little, six little pumpkins,
Seven little, eight little, nine little pumpkins,
Ten little pumpkin heads.
(Raise fingers to match the numbers up to 10, then place hands around head)

Don't Spill the Beans (Milton Bradley, A Division of Hasbro)

Farm Families (Milton Bradley, A Division of Hasbro)

Grow Garden Grow (BRIO AB Sweden, distributed by BRIO Corp.)

Hot Potato (Parker Brothers, A Division of the Tonka Corporation)

Software

Art center. (1993). San Mateo, CA: Creative Wonders.

Bailey's book house. (1993). Redmond, WA: Edmark Corporation.

Crayola art studio 2. (1995). Richardson, TX: Micrografx, Inc.

Facemaker, golden edition. (1986). Fairfield, CT: Queue.

Harry and the haunted house. (1995.) [Based on the story by Mark Schlichting, Living Books Series.] New York: Random House New Media.

Hello Kitty—Big fun deluxe. (1994). San Francisco: Big Top Productions.

Sammy's science house. (1994). Redmond, WA: Edmark Corporation.

Talking textwriter. (1986). New York: Scholastic New Media.

Trudy's time and place house. (1995). Redmond, WA: Edmark Corporation.

NOTES

NOTES

NOTES

NOTES

NOTES

NOTES

NOTES

ORDER FORM

READ, PLAY, AND LEARN! STORYBOOK ACTIVITIES FOR YOUNG CHILDREN

The Transdisciplinary Play-Based Curriculum from Toni Linder

Please send me the following:

____ **Teacher's Guide** / Stock # 4005 / $45.00

____ **Module Collection 1**
Stock # 4013 / $125.00

The Kissing Hand, by Audrey Penn
Somebody and the Three Blairs, by Marilyn Tolhurst
Picking Apples & Pumpkins, by Amy and Richard Hutchings
The Little Old Lady Who Was Not Afraid of Anything, by Linda Williams
The Knight and the Dragon, by Tomie dePaola
Night Tree, by Eve Bunting
Abiyoyo, by Pete Seeger
The Snowy Day, by Ezra Jack Keats

____ **Module Collection 2**
Stock # 4021 / $125.00

A Porcupine Named Fluffy, by Helen Lester
The Three Little Javelinas, by Susan Lowell
First Flight, by David McPhail
Franklin Has a Sleepover, by Paulette Bourgeois and Brenda Clark
Friends, by Helme Heine
The Rainbow Fish, by Marcus Pfister
The Three Billy Goats Gruff, by Janet Stevens
A Rainbow of Friends, by P.K. Hallinan

ADDITIONAL TRANDISCIPLINARY PLAY-BASED RESOURCES

Transdisciplinary Play-Based Assessment uses a play-based process with accompanying Observation Guidelines to assess a child's abilities and learning styles. Intervention guidelines in the companion volume, *Transdisciplinary Play-Based Intervention,* help individualize instruction to match each child's developmental level and personal characteristics. Forms to use with TPBA and TPBI are sold separately. Two training videotapes, developed by Toni W. Linder, are also available.

____ **Transdisciplinary Play-Based Assessment** / Stock # 1626 / $44.00
____ **Transdisciplinary Play-Based Intervention** / Stock # 1308 / $49.95
____ Order **TPBA** and **TPBI** as a **set** / Stock # OLIN / $83.95
____ **Transdisciplinary Play-Based Assessment and Intervention: Child Program Summary Forms**
Stock # 1634 / $27.00 (pkg. of 5 tablets)
____ **And You Thought They Were Just Playing** / Stock # 2223 / $175.00 / VHS videotape / 65 min.
____ **Observing Kassandra** / Stock # 2665 / $169.00 / VHS videotape / 50 min.

____ Bill my institution (purchase order must be attached)

____ Payment enclosed (make checks payable to Brookes Publishing Co.)

__ VISA __ MC __ AMEX Credit Card #: ____________ Exp. date: ____

Signature (needed for all credit card purchases): ____________

Daytime telephone: ____________

Name: ____________

Address: ____________

City/State/ZIP: ____________

Maryland orders add 5% sales tax.

Photocopy order form and send to: Brookes Publishing Co., P.O. Box 10624, Baltimore, MD 21285-0624

FAX (410) 337-8539; call toll-free (8 A.M.–5 P.M. ET) (800) 638-3775; or order on-line at **www.brookespublishing.com**

Yours to review for 30 days, risk-free. Contact Customer Service for more information on Brookes Publishing's return policy.

Prices subject to change without notice. Prices may be higher outside the United States. Source Code: BA18